The Steppe and Beyond: Studies on Central Asia

Series Editor

Jean-François Caron, Department of Political Science and International Relations, Nazarbayev University, Astana, Kazakhstan

Surrounded between Europe and Asia, Central Asia has been neglected by many experts for a very long time. Many reasons may explain this situation, such as the language barrier and the fact that the region remained inaccessible for the most part of the 20th Century. However, this situation is clearly about to change in light of the growing interest of the academic interest for this region and the purpose of this series is to enhance the understanding of this region which is has always been at the crossroad of various civilizations. From a multidisciplinary perspective, this series examines the history of the region, its past struggles with colonialism and communism as well as the political and sociological challenges Central Asian countries are currently facing with the emergence of the new Silk Road and the strategic power shift in the region. It also proposes to render accessible to English-speaking readers the important oral literary tradition of Central Asia, which is one of the largest in the world.

Jean-François Caron
Editor

A Revolt in the Steppe

Understanding Kazakhstan's January Events of 2022

palgrave
macmillan

Editor
Jean-François Caron
Nazarbayev University
Astana, Kazakhstan

ISSN 2524-8359 ISSN 2524-8367 (electronic)
The Steppe and Beyond: Studies on Central Asia
ISBN 978-981-99-0782-3 ISBN 978-981-99-0783-0 (eBook)
https://doi.org/10.1007/978-981-99-0783-0

This Palgrave Macmillan imprint is published by the registered company Springer Nature Singapore Pte Ltd.
The registered company address is: 152 Beach Road, #21-01/04 Gateway East, Singapore 189721, Singapore

Contents

Notes on Contributors

Thomas Ambrosio is a Professor of political science at North Dakota State University in Fargo, ND, USA, who researches the former Soviet Union, international relations, authoritarianism, and the critical geopolitics of boardgames. One of his most recent publications includes a study in *Europe-Asia Studies* which utilizes national security documents to examine intra-alliance security dilemmas between Russia, Belarus, and Ukraine in the wake of the 2014 Ukraine crisis.

Jean-François Caron is Associate Professor in the Department of Political Science and International Relations at Nazarbayev University. He received his Ph.D. in Political Science from Laval University (Canada) in 2010.

Akbota Karibayeva is a Ph.D. student in Political Science at the George Washington University. Her current research interests include power successions, digital authoritarianism, nationalizing ethnic regimes, and authoritarian protest management in post-Soviet states. She holds an M.A. in International Relations from the University of Chicago and a B.A. from Nazarbayev University in Astana.

Edward Lemon is a Research Assistant Professor at the Bush School of Government and Public Service at Texas A&M University and Global Fellow at the Wilson Center and President of the Oxus Society. Dr. Lemon received his Ph.D. in political science from the University of

Exeter (2016). Dr. Lemon's research focuses on the transnational dimensions of authoritarianism, including transnational repression and authoritarian regional organizations, with a focus on post-Soviet Central Asia, Russia, and China.

Nurmakhan Tastaibek is a senior undergraduate student in the department of Political science and international relations at Nazarbayev University (NU). His research interests include authoritarianism and political violence in Central Asia. He co-published a commentary, "Central Asia is crucial in 2022: Is Russia out, and is China (still) in?" in Pearls and Irritations. His experience includes research assistantship in the NU graduate school of education and involvement with the Konrad-Adenauer-Stiftung and the human rights organization Erkindik Qanaty (Wings of Liberty) in Kazakhstan.

Hélène Thibault is an associate professor in the department of Political science and international relations at Nazarbayev University (NU). She holds a Ph.D. from the University of Ottawa (2014). She is a co-investigator in the Political Economy of Education Research (PEER) Network. She specializes in issues of religion, gender, and sexuality in Central Asia. Recent publications include an edited volume, *Uyat and the Culture of Shame in Central Asia*, published with Palgrave and an article "Where did all the Wahhabis go? The evolution of threat in Central Asian scholarship" in *Europe-Asia Studies*.

An Unpredictable Revolt in the Steppe?

Jean-François Caron

Abstract These introductory remarks are discussing the evolution of Kazakhstani politics from the resignation of Nursultan Nazarbayev in March 2019 until the January events of 2022 as well as summarizing the book's chapters.

Keyword Kazakhstan · Nursultan Nazarbayev · Kassym-Jomart Tokayev

In early January 2022, Kazakhstan faced unexpected mass protests against the sudden sharp increase of the price of liquefied gas. If these protests were peaceful at first, they quickly turned violent especially in Almaty and in other cities in the Southern part of the country. Government buildings were seized by protestors before they were set on fire, arms depots were looted and Almaty's international airport was vandalized. This situation prompted its President to impose the state of emergency

J.-F. Caron (✉)
Nazarbayev University, Astana, Kazakhstan
e-mail: jean-francois.caron@nu.edu.kz

J.-F. Caron (ed.), *A Revolt in the Steppe*, The Steppe and Beyond: Studies on Central Asia,
https://doi.org/10.1007/978-981-99-0783-0_1

throughout the country, to shut down the internet for days, to order the police/military forces "to shoot to kill" and to call upon the support of other members of the Collective Security Treaty Organization to deploy their troops in Kazakhstan. The immediate consequences of these troubles were considerable. Officially, more than 200 people were killed (including 19 members of the security forces, some of whom were apparently beheaded) and nearly 10,000 protesters were arrested. For its part, the Atameken business lobby estimated that the looting that resulted from these events impacted more than 1,700 business that suffered losses of more than 220 million USD, while the Kazakhstani government estimated to 3 billion USD the total cost of the crisis. For a moment, what was thought by many to be the most politically stable country of Central Asia was trembling.

Aside from these human and economic costs, these tragic events also triggered tremendous political changes that nobody dared to predict only a few weeks before they happened. Indeed, back in March 2019, few people thought that the resignation of Nursultan Nazarbayev who had been ruling Kazakhstan since its independence in 1991 would allow his successor Kassym-Jomart Tokayev any genuine margin of freedom. As many believed at the time, the bicephalous form of executive that came out of this unexpected transition would allow *Elbasy*'s—Nazarbayev's title as "leader of the nation" that was bestowed on him in 2010 by Parliament—capacity to keep the upper hand on the management of the country he had ruled with an iron first for almost 30 years. Indeed, despite resigning as Head of Kazakhstan, Nazarbayev kept enormous powers by remaining the Chairman of the country's Security Council, the Head of the Presidential party (*Nur-Otan*) that controls Kazakhstan's Parliament as well as a member of the Constitutional Council. In addition to these powers, it was also widely assumed that Tokayev—who had always been known for being a close allied of Nazarbayev—would simply act as a token Head of state who would not challenge the internal dynamic of the system his predecessor had patiently put in place. In support of this belief, amendments to the power of the President[1] were approved in October 2019 by Tokayev that forced him to obtain Nazarbayev's agreement for the nomination of most cabinet ministers (except for the

[1] О внесении изменений и дополнений в некоторые акты Президента Республики Казахстан, October 9, 2019. http://adilet.zan.kz/rus/docs/U1900000184.

ministers of foreign affairs, defense, and internal affairs), regional governors, the secret services (KNB), members of the Prosecutor General's Office, and members of his security detail.

Nobody expected that less than three years later Tokayev would strip Nazarbayev of all his positions, replace the Prime Minister he inherited from him,[2] and arrest some of his closest allies under charges of high treason—such as Karim Massimov, who was at the time of the January events the Head of the KNB[3]—or (to use a euphemism) "force into resignation" direct members of Nazarbayev's family. More precisely, his eldest daughter, Dariga, resigned from her seat in Parliament in February 2022, while her rumored husband,[4] Kairat Sharipbaev, resigned as chief executive of natural-gas pipeline QazaqGaz. For their part, the husband of Nazarbayev's second daughter's, the very powerful Timur Kulibayev, resigned as Chairman of the country's main business lobby group, alongside his third daughter's husband, Dimash Dosanov, who relinquished his position of CEO of the state oil pipeline firm KazTransOil. The state also took control of the lucrative recycling company owned by Nazarbayev's third daughter, Aliya. All-in-all, in the course of only a few weeks, the powerful of yesterday lost everything and were pushed into exile as an abundant number of private jets flying out of Kazakhstan during the January events were suggesting that family members of Nazarbayev were fleeing the country, such as his notorious brother, Bolat, who allegedly crossed the Kyrgyz border by car before boarding a plane in direction of Dubai (Pannier, 2022).[5] The final page of the "de-Nazarbayevification"

[2] Following Nazarbayev's resignation, Askar Mamin remained Head of the government until January 2022 when he was replaced by Alikhan Smailov.

[3] Who was replaced by Yermek Sagimbayev, whom Tokayev had previously appointed himself as Head of his security service.

[4] https://rus.azattyq.org/a/the-big-family-of-nursultan-nazarbayev/30977086.html.

[5] It is interesting to note that of all those names were evoked as possible future head of state by Central Asianists in the aftermath of Nazarbayev's resignation have all been sidelined ever since (Lemon, 2019). This has been the case with Karim Massimov, Dariga Nazarbayeva, and Timur Kulibayev for the aforementioned reasons, but also for Kairat Satybaldy and Samat Abish—two of Nazarbayev's nephews who have either been arrested following the January events (Satybaldy) or dismissed from their positions (in the case of Abish who served as Massimov's deputy)—and Imangali Tasmagambetov (a former mayor of Astana and Almaty, Minister of Defense, Prime Minister, and ambassador of Kazakhstan to Russia) who was dismissed from public service and sent into retirement by Tokayev in December 2019.

process was first turned on June 5, 2022, following a referendum that led to the modification of about a third of the country's constitution, which included such measures like the stripping of Nazarbayev's title of "leader of the nation" and the loss of all his privileges that came with it, including full immunity against prosecution for his family.[6] Secondly, only a few months later, it was announced that the capital would be renamed Astana after it was named "Nur-Sultan" in March 2019 following the resignation of Nazarbayev.

In retrospect, some events that preceded the January events should have raised concerns over the solidity of the bounds between Tokayev and Nazarbayev. For instance, Dariga Nazarbayeva was suddenly dismissed from her position of Chair of the Senate on May 2, 2020: a position that was putting her in direct succession to Tokayev in the event of his resignation, death, or incapacity to govern the country. She was replaced by Maulen Ashimbayev, a loyalist of Tokayev, and prompted a game of musical chairs that led other allies of the President to be moved or promoted to key positions within the government. Furthermore, as I had indicated in the introduction of the book I edited on the 2019 transition, the leaking of documents regarding the financial activities of two of Nazarbayev's most loyal allies, namely Bulat Utemuratov and Timur Kulibayev, was surprising in a country where the elites had always closed ranks and was probably indicating nascent conflicts in the corridors of power in Astana (Caron, 2021, p. 5).

Accordingly, the question that will most likely remain unanswered is whether members of Nazarbayev's clan played either an active or a supporting role in the organization of the January events in order to overthrow Tokayev from power because of his unwillingness to play the part he was expected to follow or if Tokayev simply instrumentalized these events to blame the old guard and clean the stable in order to solidify his own grip on power so he could implement his own political agenda without fearing interferences from hostile and unfaithful elites. This book will not go into speculations of these sorts, but will rather try to have an objective view of these events based on existing literature as well as exploring questions and challenges that are related to these events.

[6] He only kept his as a former Kazakhstani President according to the country's constitution.

In this chapter, Jean-François Caron offers an overview of how other Central Asian republics and other states have managed their political transitions (whether "planned" or "mortuary"). In light of these numerous case studies, he is trying to identify the main factors that have contributed to what we can now call the "de-Nazarbayevification" process. As he is arguing, despite his longevity in office, the transition model chosen in 2019 was not the most conducive to the perpetuation of Nazarbayev's legacy which was in fact built upon very weak foundations that made it highly vulnerable to criticisms. However, despite being able to quickly reestablish peace and order following a very tumultuous start of 2022, the fact remains that the problems that contributed to the January events and the marginalization of the Nazarbayev clan have not been solved at all, meaning that the current regime's ability to legitimize its actions is still hugely problematic.

Secondly, if Kazakhstan's foreign policy of multivectorism that has consisted in building ties with its neighbors and other powerful blocks (namely the United States and the European Union) was already problematic before the January events, needless to say that the Russia-led CSTO intervention in the country as well as the invasion of Ukraine by Russian forces one month later have put the country into a new political dynamic. As Thomas Ambrosio argues, although the CSTO intervention did not put Astana in Moscow's debt as it was highlighted by Astana remaining neutral in the conflict (and even by distancing itself from Moscow), 2022 has nonetheless shown the high dependency of Kazakhstan with its Northern neighbor which could manifest itself in various ways in the following years: a fear fueled by an irredentist rhetoric on the part of top-Russian officials. In this regard, Tokayev's decision to call on Russia and the CSTO to help him during the January events may sooner rather than later result in the chickens coming home to roost and hinder Astana's independence.

In Chapter "Between Threat, Alliance, and Multivectorism: Kazakh-Russian Relations in the Wake of the Russo-Ukrainian War", Akbota Karibayeva and Edward Lemon are exploring the reputational costs the January events had on Kazakhstan and how the government framed them in order to maintain its legitimacy over its population. Indeed, by virtually shutting down all internet and mobile phone networks in the midst of the protests, by ordering the police forces to shoot-to-kill without warning and by calling on the CSTO to intervene, the government could have easily lost its legitimacy among the Kazakhstani people. In what could very well become a *cas d'école* for other authoritarian states, Karibayeva and Lemon are discussing how the government managed to justify the exceptional measures taken, how the narrative shifted over time, and how the it tried to spin events in a positive way in order to reinforce the regime and reduce the post-factum audience costs of repression.

In the same vein, Hélène Thibault and Nurmakhan Tastaibek are further exploring in the last chapter of this book how the labeling of protesters as terrorists allowed the Kazakhstani government to legitimize its actions. Although composed by a majority of Muslims, Kazakhstan has nonetheless remained largely secular since it gained its independence and its citizens' involvement in extremist groups has remained a marginal feature ever since. This fear of Islamic radicalization has nonetheless haunted the minds of political leaders, especially following terrorist attacks in Aktobe and in Almaty in 2016 as well as the fact that hundreds of Kazakhstanis joined the *Jihad* in Syria alongside the forces of the Islamic State. As a result, Thibault and Tastaibek are arguing that Islamic terrorism has become the usual scapegoat whenever troubles are arising in the region (the phenomenon has also been observed in the other "Stans") and a tool of choice to delegitimize popular protests, to hide the real nature of people's frustrations and demands and to justify the harsh measures used by governments.

References

Caron, J.-F. (Ed.). (2021). *Understanding Kazakhstan's 2019 Political Transition*. Springer.

Lemon, E. (2019, March 20). *Why Nazarbayev Resigned and What Happens Next*? https://www.wilsoncenter.org/blog-post/why-nazarbayev-resigned-and-what-happens-next

Pannier, B. (2022, January 12). *The Campaign Against Nazarbaev and the Cronies of Kazakhstan's First President Has Begun*. Radio Free Europe. https://www.rferl.org/a/kazakhstan-nazarbaev-cronies-Tokayev/31651330.html

Will You Preserve My Political Legacy? Lessons from Kazakhstan and Other Authoritarian States

Jean-François Caron

Abstract The January events of 2022 resulted in an outcome that was unexpected when Nursultan Nazarbayev resigned as President in March 2019. While everything was pointing in the direction of a perpetuation of his legacy and his capacity to maintain his grip on state's affairs, these events led to a "de-Nazarbayevification" process that saw him lose his honorary title and his constitutional protections, the renaming of the capital from "Nur-Sultan" back to Astana as well as a purge among his closest allies and family members. By looking at other cases of succession in authoritarian countries, this chapter tries to identify the main factors that can explain what has been one of the major outcomes of the January events.

Keywords Elite Divide · Authoritarianism · Transition · Legacy

---

J.-F. Caron (✉)
Nazarbayev University, Astana, Kazakhstan
e-mail: jean-francois.caron@nu.edu.kz

J.-F. Caron (ed.), *A Revolt in the Steppe*, The Steppe and Beyond: Studies on Central Asia,
https://doi.org/10.1007/978-981-99-0783-0_2

For individuals living in states where a Weberian rational-legal logic of legitimacy prevails, political succession is usually not a problem.[1] When citizens and politicians are willing to abide by the democratic rules of their constitutional order, the choice of the next Prime Minister or President follows a clearly defined pattern and everybody agrees—which include both those who have won the elections and those who have been defeated—that the new individual in charge possesses the required legitimacy to pursue his political goals. On paper, many authoritarian states are following a similar pattern, since their constitutions are usually indicating who ought to succeed to the Head of State in the event of his death, resignation, or incapacity to govern. This is the case, for instance, with article 96 of the Uzbek Constitution or with article 60 of the 2003 Turkmen Constitution that, respectively, stipulate that the Chair of the Senate ought to succeed the Head of State either until new presidential elections are held within a period of three months or to the Chairman of Parliament which was unicameral until 2020 in the latter case.

However, in reality, these constitutional dispositions are very often ignored. Despite not being Chair of the Senate (but Prime Minister), Shavkat Mirziyoyev was nonetheless appointed interim President of Uzbekistan until general elections confirmed him in his position. The same happened with Gurbanguly Berdimuhamedov following the death of his predecessor in 2007. While the country's presidential powers should have been transferred to Öwezgeldi Atayew for a maximum period of two months until elections could be held, Berdimuhamedov (who was then deputy Prime Minister and Minister of Health) was nonetheless chosen by the State Security Council as interim President (he also had Atayew arrested). Furthermore, while article 60 of the Constitution should have barred him from running in the anticipatory presidential elections, this disposition was simply lifted by Parliament which allowed him to rule the country with an iron fist until his resignation in 2022.

This is why political succession in authoritarian states is highly unpredictable and generally a guessing game among observers when it is happening. Not knowing what is going on behind the closed doors of this regime, analysts are left to make assumptions based on the old Soviet logic of who is in charge of the funerals or who is holding the casket of the deceased ruler. But, at the end of the day, it all comes down to

[1] I say "usually", since the 2021 riots on Capitol Hill in Washington D.C. are evidence that political succession can sometimes be violently challenged in democracies.

the obscure maneuvers of members of the elites who may even ignore the wishes of the previous ruler, as it was the case with Lenin who had warned other members of the Politburo in his testament about Stalin's capacities to take over the reins of Soviet Union.[2]

Although the 2019 transition in Kazakhstan following the resignation of Nursultan Nazarbayev followed the prescribed constitutional path,[3] many questions remained at the time. The accession to the presidency of Kassym-Jomart Tokayev did not stop many analysts to argue that he would simply be an interim Head of State before choosing to turn over his powers to Nazarbayev's eldest daughter, Dariga, who was promoted Speaker of the Senate by Tokayev's in his first decision as President, thereby making her his automatic successor in the eventually of his death, resignation or incapacity to govern. With this move, a newspaper article stated that "Kazakhstan [had taken] a step closer to a carefully choreographed dynastic succession" (Reuters, 2019). How wrong analysts were when they made that prediction! As it turned out, Tokayev managed in less than three years to erase almost the entirety of his predecessor's legacy by removing all of his allies from key positions and by withdrawing his title of "leader of the nation" (*Elbasy*) which had been bestowed on him in 2010. Furthermore, as the time of writing this chapter, the Kazakhstani Parliament was studying a bill that would not only abolish the legal immunity originally granted to his family members,[4] but also the budget that the government allocates to expenses related to the maintenance of his "First President" organization, namely housing, transport, a museum, a personal archive, a personal library, and medical assistance (Sorbello, 2022). In fact, this rejection has been so severe, that it has even be labeled a "de-Nazarbayevification" process. Consequently, this chapter will try to determine what may be the reasons behind the failure of Nazarbayev's succession strategy and the rapid erosion of his legacy by looking primarily at the factors that are usually associated with the perpetuation of a political legacy in authoritarian regimes and by

[2] He even suggested that he be removed from his office of General Secretary.

[3] In accordance with article 48(1), Kassym-Jomart Tokayev who was at the time Speaker of the Senate, automatically assumed the functions of President.

[4] As a former President, he would nonetheless keep his immunity as stated in the country's constitution.

comparing the Kazakhstani case with the 1990 transition in Singapore: an example that shares a lot of similarities with the 2019 Kazakhstani transition.

A Typology of Political Succession in Authoritarian States and Their Fate: Factors Contributing to the Continuation or a *Tabula Rasa* of the Predecessor's Legacy?

Authoritarian leaders are facing two challenges. The first one is being able to remain in power during their lifetime and to avoid being ousted by a popular revolution (or by a palace revolution (or by being able to fix themselves the moment and terms of their retirement). In order to achieve this, leaders have to be able to brilliantly balance in a Machiavellian manner the various interests of the elites and those of the people in a way where everybody will be able to benefit from the regime (Caron, 2019a). In other words, they need to be able to generate enough repression that will suppress the opposition, but not in an excessive and irrational way, otherwise this would hinder their capacity to successfully co-opt the elites and to legitimize their rule as being one that is perceived as favorable to the general interest (Gerschewski, 2013). In many places, nepotism or an excessive degree of repression has prevented elite co-optation and has generated an internal oppositional dynamic between the grievances of the repressed people and the deposed elite who became unable to enrich themselves. When this is the case, an authoritarian leader becomes inherently fragile and susceptible to face a regime change (Caron & Malikova, 2021; McAdam et al., 2001). Just like high-wire walkers, they can only owe their fate to their own *virtu* that consists in the uneasy task of balancing everybody's opposite interests.

For its part, the second challenge is related to the preservation or the erosion of their political legacy. Once, they have relinquished voluntarily their position of Head of State or once they are dead, this destiny is completely out of their hands and depends entirely on the goodwill of their successor. In the case of Central Asia, if many authoritarian leaders have been able for the most part to successfully meet the first challenge, we cannot say the same about the second one. Generally speaking, two different patterns have emerged over the last 30 years in the region with variable degree of success when it comes to the continuation of the previous Head of State's legacy. They are:

1. The "planned transition" where the Head of State chooses his successor before resigning from his position. This has been the case in Azerbaijan in 2003, as well as Kazakhstan in 2019 and more recently in Turkmenistan in 2022 (we can also add the case of Russia where Boris Yelstin carefully handpicked Vladimir Putin as his successor before resigning from office in 1999 and when the latter chose Dmitri Medvedev to succeed him for one term in 2008);
2. The "mortuary transition" that follows the unexpected death of the previous ruler. This has been the case in Turkmenistan in 2006 and in Uzbekistan in 2016 when Saparmurat Niyazov and Islam Karimov both died in office.

Both of these models are sometimes associated with a sub-pattern, that is the "family/dynastic transition" model where the previous leader is succeeded by one of his family members, usually one of his sons. This has been the case in Azerbaijan in 2003 as well as in Turkmenistan in 2022 after Gurbanguly Berdimuhamedov was succeeded by his son, Serdar, following his resignation on March 19. It is also largely assumed that this sub-pattern will happen in Tajikistan as the current ruler Emomali Rahmon seems to be grooming his son Rustam to succeed him either after his resignation or his death (Lemon, 2021, p. 68). All-in-all, it seems as if this sub-pattern is the most conducive to the preservation of a former leader's legacy whether his departure from power resulted from one of the two dominant patterns.

Indeed, none of these two models have proved themselves successful in preserving the predecessor's legacy when they were not associated with the "sub-pattern" of family/dynastic transition. As it has already been described, although his first few months in office showed no signs of defiance to Nazarbayev[5] or differences in his successor's methods of governance, especially his way of dealing with protesters, it took barely three years for Tokayev to detach himself from his predecessor's legacy by removing his allies from power, to abolish his constitutional safeguards

[5] In fact, he openly said in his first annual address to the nation that he would maintain the continuity of the policy of his predecessor (Akorda, 2019).

that prevented him from being prosecuted and by openly calling for a democratization of the regime (although this promise remains currently at the rhetorical stage).

In Turkmenistan, the sudden death of Niyazov in December 2006 and the accession to power of Berdimuhamedov has also led not only to a quick halt to the former impressive personality cult by ordering the removal of the numerous portraits and monuments of his predecessor in towns and cities[6] and also restored the original names of the month he had renamed after himself and his mother (a personality cult that was, it must be said, replaced by one dedicated to the new ruler in ways that are very similar to the one of Niyazov[7]), but he also openly admitted in a lecture in 2007 at Columbia University that his predecessor had left behind a lot of problems and did not hesitate to purge members of Niyazov's inner circle among whom many were instrumental to his own rise to power (Lemon, 2021, pp. 61–62).

The death of Islam Karimov in Uzbekistan followed a similar pattern (minus the Turkmenistan-type extreme personality cult). His successor, Shavkat Mirziyoyev, quickly removed from their position the other two individuals who were listed as potential successors to Karimov, namely Finance Minister Rustam Azimov and the powerful head of the National Security Service, Rustam Inoyatov. He also launched an attack against the Ministry of Justice and the office of the Prosecutor General by calling some of their influential members as "the biggest thieves of the old rotten system" (Lemon, 2021, p. 63) as well as initiated a partial dismantlement of Karimov's dictatorship through a series of Liberal reforms in virtually

[6] The most famous being the so-called Arch of Neutrality that consisted in a 15 meters rotating gold-plated statue of Niyazov on a 75 meters marble-covered plinth in the country's capital, Ashgabat, that was always facing the sun.

[7] Berdimuhamedov also named streets and state buildings after his relatives. For instance, he turned into a museum the office his father used to have at his police unit. Some of his personal belongings have also been transformed into holy relics, such as a guitar he once used to play a song on national television that is now in display in a state museum (Najibullah, 2012). Rafael Sattarov wrote, "Berdimuhamedov has removed everything that reminds him of his predecessor. The presidential palace is new, the monuments are new, and the cult of personality is also new—even the obedience rituals are new. Instead of kissing the leader's ring as under Niyazov, Turkmen officials now kneel before Berdimuhamedov when receiving awards. Berdimuhamedov has replaced one cult of blind obedience, in which he was a supplicant, with another, in which he receives all the personal glory" (Sattarov, 2018).

every aspect of the country's life (Human Rights Watch, 2019; Starr & Cornell, 2018; Voices of Central Asia, 2017).

In return, it appears like these two patterns are more conducive to the preservation of the former leader's legacy when they are associated with the family/dynastic model sub-pattern based upon the sole example in the region with a long-enough experience that allows us to make such a judgment, that is the case of Azerbaijan (because the 2022 transition in Turkmenistan between Gurbanguly Berdimuhamedov and his son is still recent, it is premature to make any valuable evaluation at the moment). In the Azerbaijani case, because of his failing health, Heydar Aliyev resigned from power in October 2003 a few weeks before his death and appointed his son, Ilham, as the sole candidate of his party for the presidential elections that were constitutionally required. Despite being dead for almost 20 years now, Heydar Aliyev remains a central figure in the national narrative of Azerbaijan and is depicted as the father of the nation (the equivalent to the figure of *Ataturk* in Turket). Although Ilham had plenty of time to overtake his father's role during his tenure at the head of the country, he has rather decided to remain in his shadow.

Many factors can explain this attitude that has been favorable to the continuity of the predecessor's legacy. We can argue that the Freudian refusal to kill one's father may be at cause here (who knows). But what seems to be the most plausible explanation is related to Ilham's inexperience as a politician when he took over her father's position thanks to nepotism and not because of his talents (unlike his father). This latter factor may explain why Ilham has decided to simply pursue his father's policies as a way to solidify the foundations of his own reign and provide him with the legitimacy he needed. As of today, calling upon his legacy—referred to as "Heydarism"—remains a common occurrence. For instance, in May 2022, a presidential aide emphasized the fact that Heydar Aliyev's legacy was being preserved and that all government's actions were in line with his vision, including what he called the liberation of the Karabakh region from Armenia in 2020 (Azernews, 2022). The same can be said in the case of Serdar Berdimuhamedov whose young age and lack of experience in managing high stakes questions are not really allowing him to pursue his own course of action[8] (alongside the

[8] After becoming President, he did not change his father's last cabinet (apart from nominating one new member who took over the position he had before his election).

fact that his father remains an important political figure as Chairperson of the People's Council of Turkmenistan, the country's senate).

But, we also need to wonder whether or not the family/dynastic pattern is really a determinant factor to consider? Maybe the successor's willingness to preserve his predecessor's legacy can be explained differently and in a way where the genetic connections are not playing a role at all. At the end of the day, we must be open to the idea that this factor may be misleading and totally irrelevant. There are indeed numerous advantages in not questioning the legacy of one's predecessor and the most important one is certainly the message it is sending to the elites, especially when they are united and largely supportive of maintaining the status quo. Indeed, if they were able to benefit from the political/economic order instituted by the previous ruler, the willingness of his successor not to criticize it and to preserve it brings for them the guarantee that their well-being will not be hindered, hereby keeping the elites happy and united: a key element for political stability in authoritarian states. An unassured and inexperience leader—especially a "Prince of *fortuna*"—may simply see in the continuity with the past the most secure path to keep power (with all the perks that come with it). In other words, hereditary succession's main advantage is the fact that it lies upon the assumption that the previous political arrangements will remain unscathed and, accordingly, the elites will tend to rally around the heir who is assumed to be the defender rather than the denier of his father's legacy. Furthermore, in the case of an inexperienced ruler, the elite believes that they will be able to have influence over him and to sway some decisions in their favor. Ultimately, this option is far better than a palace revolution that may simply lead unexpectedly to regime change or an unconstrained power struggle between opponents that might end up endangering their current position. Similar experiences have happened and have been successful elsewhere for this precise reason (Brownlee, 2007, p. 616).

In return, challenging the status quo or initiating talks about how the previous regime was "corrupted" or "rotten" invariably bring uncertainties for those who have benefitted from it in the past, especially if this rhetoric is associated with a strong or significant popular wave of support. This could be made possible or easier when the elites are not keeping a united front, especially between those who were the inevitable minority close to the inner circle of the previous ruler and the others who were still able to enrich themselves albeit to a lesser degree than the former. Such an internal tension is very often the roots of serious political problems in an authoritarian state: a tension that can simply be used by those who are benefitting to a lesser extent when the large-scale political corruption is perceived by the population as hindering their own interests. In such cases, striking against those who have benefitted the most from the previous regime (and who are inevitably composing a smaller group than those who have not enjoyed a similar abundance) becomes a tempting option for the new ruler who may see this as an opportunity to solidify his reign by pleasing the people and a majority of disgruntled members of the elite who will feel that a *tabula rasa* may open up new opportunities for them or put an end to the previously unfair system they were jealous of.

It must be noted that Nazarbayev's regime faced this type of elite divide between 2001 and 2007, but managed to calm things down by being able to find a fine balance between fear and concession. As mentioned by numerous authors (e.g., Lillis, 2018; Kjaenet et al., 2008; Junisbai, 2010), Nazarbayev's reign was marked by the control that the members of his inner circle, namely his daughters and his sons-in-law (Timur Kulibaev and Rakhat Aliev, Dariga Nazarbayeva's first husband), gained over the oil and gas sectors. However, such a concentration of resources in the hands of a few would be detrimental to the regime's stability, as it would frustrate others from enriching themselves. Therefore, the control over how the Kazakh economy is organized can metaphorically resemble the solar system: it is composed of different entities that gradually lose their influence as they move away from the sun (represented by Nazarbayev). If the development of an inner circle, which is intimately connected with the head of state, is made possible through economic statism, the appearance of other planets revolving around the sun is made possible thanks to Kazakhstan's economic liberalization after the collapse of Soviet Union which allowed businessmen and entrepreneurs to build-up their fortunes independently from political power, and that was reserved for the members of the inner circle, despite being cut-off from the economic sectors.

In the 2000s, there were some tensions within the business sector when the inner circle became too greedy (Ahrens et al., 2016). In particular, Rakhat Aliev tried to expand his control over other economic sectors by forcing other businessmen to sell their companies below their value through various schemes (Junisbai, 2010, pp. 248–249). Fearing for their own ability to prosper, the second-tier elites formed a protest movement called the *Demokraticheskii Vybor Kazakhstana*.[9] Nazarbayev reacted quickly and decisively by punishing the representatives of the inner circle for creating such problems. Aliev was demoted from his position in the government and was informed about his divorce from Dariga Nazarbayeva by fax. Kulibaev, who was deputy chair of the Samruk Fund (the biggest state holding which controls the gas and oil sectors), was also removed from his position. For her part, Dariga Nazarbayeva lost her TV channel and was removed from the party list of *Nur-Otan*. With the support of Kassym-Jomart Tokayev, who was the Prime Minister at the time, Nazarbayev launched investigations into the members of the second-tier elites who had been very vocal against the regime.[10] These measures led at the time to a compromise between the two groups: if the second-tier elites received the clear message that they were not entitled access to all the privileges that the members of the inner circle possessed, they would also receive the guarantee that the latter would no longer try to interfere with their businesses.

In light of how swiftly Tokayev managed to remove from their positions those who used to be the closest to the sun, according to the aforementioned metaphor, and how he openly criticized them on January 11, 2022, in a televised speech,[11] we can wonder if the country was not experiencing a revival of the elite divide that had previously shaken the foundations of Nazarbayev's reign and a growing resentment on the part of the second-tier elites toward the immensely rich members of the inner circle. These tensions may have led Tokayev to strike in favor of the majority of disgruntled elite in order to preserve his rule and by taking advantage of the clear and strong dissatisfaction of the population that also openly criticized during the January events Nazarbayev's cronyism and the deep inequalities it created since 1991.[12]

[9] According to Junisbai and Junisbai (2005, p. 12), the creation of this movement resulted from an opposition to "the existing clientelistic or patrimonial system rather than the expression of competition between clans or other traditional forms of social cleavages."

[10] Main leaders of the opposition movement were investigated and sentenced for economic fraud and corruption or were killed under strange circumstances. Others had to liquidate their assets or were stripped of them.

[11] In which he said: "Thanks to the first president, Elbasy, a group of very profitable companies emerged in the country, as well as a group of people whose wealth is significant even by international standards" (Pannier, 2022).

[12] A statue of Nazarbayev being toppled in the city of Taldyqorghan in a way similar to those of Saddam Hussein in 2003 was recorded and largely diffused online.

Comparing Kazakhstan 2019 Transition with Singapore

In many ways, the Kazakhstani political transition of 2019 was very similar to the one that occurred in another illiberal state, namely Singapore after the city-state's founding father, Lee Kwan Yew, resigned from power (Burkhanov et al., 2021). Although his duties of Prime Minister were transferred to Goh Chok Tong who promised to Singaporeans to continue Yew's legacy (Kim, 1991, p. 173), Yew nonetheless kept an advisory role as a member of the Cabinet thanks to his title of "Senior Minister." Nazarbayev's decision to follow a similar path was no stranger to the admiration he openly manifested in favor of the founder of Singapore by referring to him, along with Charles de Gaulle, as one of two "eminent founding statesmen" worth emulating, while stating that he also had a similar plan to step down from power, while still retaining important functions within the regime (Michel, 2015). However, contrary to what happened to Nazarbayev, Yew's legacy has remained vivid and celebrated in the country following his resignation and his death in 2015. How can we explain these two different fates?

Despite the obvious similarities between Singapore and Kazakhstan, we cannot neglect their profound differences that may have explained the separate fate of the legacy of their founding fathers. The readers must be aware that what has been argued previously remains largely speculative and it is impossible to be certain—although various elements tend to give weight to that hypothesis—that a possible elite divide may have led to the growing tensions between members of Nazarbayev's inner circle and the other members of the elite who may have felt disenfranchised from the deal made between them some 15 years before. This theory presupposes that Kazakhstan was indeed victim of a palace revolution of the former who tried to re-consolidate their power and influence that was slipping away from them or that President Tokayev took advantage of the massive protests to show his support to the people by striking against those who were widely known for having accumulated obscene fortunes thanks to Nazarbayev's klepto-patrimonial regime, with the result of leaving the rest of the population with an average monthly income of 627 USD[13] (as of April 2022). If the first theory cannot be proved, the second one is nonetheless highlighting a very serious problem that may

[13] https://www.ceicdata.com/en/indicator/kazakhstan/monthly-earnings.

have contributed to Tokayev being forced to distance himself from the Nazarbayev's legacy in hope of appearing like a well-needed reformer the people were asking for and to prevent the country from falling into an anarchic and mobbish state of nature (Caron, 2019b).

Whether it was or not his intention to distance himself from the legacy of his predecessor, his own political survival required him to opt for the *tabula rasa* option after only a relatively small increase of the price of a commodity led thousands of people to protest and make demands for massive political changes. This was not the case in Singapore upon Yew's resignation. Indeed, this city-state never experienced any organized opposition movement demanding greater freedom or any other democratic reform and its people has continuously accepted the country's repressive political system and the domination of the People's Action Party (PAP) implemented by Yew and that perpetuated itself after his resignation.

The secret of Singapore's model lied on its focus on promoting the emergence of a strong middle class[14] that has been able to satisfy its material needs (Lam, 1999), thereby transforming them primarily as "consumers" rather than "citizens" (Rodan, 1992). This is why "the majority of the middle class prefers the PAP to stay in power despite its authoritarian tendencies insofar as the party continues to satisfy their material needs" (Lam, 1999, p. 274). This latter consideration was made possible thanks to their very generous salaries that now greatly explains why the people's median monthly income is now 4,680 USD: a number that is nowhere near the one found in Kazakhstan.

Furthermore, the Singapore model lies upon an important premise that is also lacking in Kazakhstan, which is becoming a happy member of the middle class—and, consequently an individual willing to subordinate his/her freedom to the principle of consumerism and to support the status quo—through a genuine form of meritocracy. Indeed, and like it has been summarized by Keiko T. Tamura:

> Singapore highly selective education is impartial at its start, meaning that the opportunity to receive an education is open to all children and students. But there-after the course of a student's education is determined

[14] This has been made possible through an industrial policy that started at the end of the 1970s that modernized the country and encouraged businesses to encourage the use of high-technology (the state expanded the educational offering in this domain) and to transfer their low-tech labor-intensive operations abroad.

> by test results. Some are compelled to leave school after receiving only a primary education; others finish up to the first part of secondary school, while others advance up to institutions of higher education. It would be no exaggeration to say that this highly selective system of education largely determines the future jobs and income of the country's children while they are still students between ten and fifteen years of age. Student with excellent grades are provided with large government scholarships and receive preferential treatment. All this has made education a paramount concern for the people. Top-level students who make up the educated elite are envied, admired, and held up for emulation. (2003, pp. 189–190)

What this means is the development of a psyche that lies on the idea that one's wealth is not the result of corruption but of merit and, as a result, prevents the development of a sense of victimization and envy among those who are not enjoying the same level of wealth and opportunities. On the contrary, peoples' professional fate is rather perceived with a sense of fatality deriving from the efforts and dedication they've put forward and their natural talent. It is therefore hard for individuals to feel that their destiny is the result of having been treated unjustly. This feeling is coupled with the fact that Singapore is one of the least corrupt society in the world with a score of 85 for the 2021 Transparency International (TI) Corruption Perceptions Index (CPI), which allowed the city-state to be ranked the 4th least corrupt nation in the world (out of 180 countries), tied with Sweden and Norway. Things are completely different in Kazakhstan which had a CPI score of 37 in 2021 and ranked as the 102nd least corrupt country. Concretely, this means that personal enrichment is not meritocratic and access to certain well-paid jobs depends upon personal connections and is not merit-based. Contrary to Singapore, such a situation tends to generate envy and resentment among the general population who are seeing the commonwealth being highjacked by undeserving and, very often, unqualified individuals whose sole notable feat is their membership to *Nur-Otan* (Isaacs, 2013).

Consequently, when 0.001% of the Kazakhstani people (or the equivalent of 162 people) is reported to be in possession of 55% of all the country's wealth (as of 2018), it becomes hard to find a strong group that will form the backbone of the regime's support among the population and a willingness on their part to embrace political continuity. In fact, despite its theoretical control over its people during all these years, Kazakhstan's authoritarianism was in fact hanging by a thread and what it took was simply a sudden increase in the price of liquefied gas (from

60 to 120 tenge, or from 0.14$ to 0.28$) to generate a strong anti-regime reaction that ultimately culminated into violence and required the intervention of foreign troops of the Collective Security Treaty Organization. To use a well-known Marxist expression, the Kazakhstani people had nothing to lose but their chains (or, to put it in terms of 2022, their credit card balance) contrary to Singaporeans following the resignation of their founding father in 1990 who had genuine reasons to treat him and his legacy with deference.

Conclusion

Alongside his former Soviet counterparts Saparmurat Niyazov and Islam Karimov, Nursultan Nazarbayev may have been able to hold on to power following the collapse of USSR as Head of one of its former republics, but he has not been able to see his legacy remain intact following his voluntary departure from power (unlike the two former leaders whose death allowed them to be spared that spectacle). In the course of less than three years, he has lost his symbolic title and his remaining powers as well as his constitutional protections (while also witnessing the political downfall of his immediate family). Two main thesis may explain this situation. If one is impossible to prove without insights and testimonies from people within the government, the second one is easier to evaluate based upon the transitional model of Singapore which had always been hailed by Nazarbayev as an example to follow. If he was expecting a treatment similar to the one Lee Kwan Yew received after his resignation as Prime Minister of the city-state and his death in 2015, Nazarbayev did not left behind the necessary and required foundations for regime continuity in an authoritarian environment. Like his regime, he proved himself to be an idol with feet of clay whose legacy was essentially blown away for a matter of 0.14$ and who went from being known as Elbasy to a normal pensioner (*пенсионер*).

This being said, his successor's capacity to successfully bring things to normal after a very tumultuous start of 2022 has not resulted in altering in any way the deep problems of the Kazakhstani state. If the country's stability turned out to be a fragile house of cards despite what many people believed prior to the January events, it still remains vulnerable to the slightest contingency. Indeed, the huge inequalities between people and the current ruling class remain very significant and are exposing the regime to further protests in the future especially if the new guard has simply copied the *modus operandi* of the old one. In return, if Tokayev ever decides to change the status quo he ought to know that he is exposing himself to potential challenges from the new elite who may see this initiative as a threat to their privileges. Only time will tell how Tokayev will face this Gordian knot until his term as President is due to expire in the Fall of 2029.

References

Ahrens, J., Hoen, H. W., & Spechler, M. C. (2016). State Capitalism in Eurasia: A Dual-Economy Approach to Central Asia. In M. Brusis, J. Ahrens & M. S. Wessel (Eds.), *Politics and Legitimacy in Post-Soviet Eurasia* (pp. 47–71). Palgrave Macmillan.

Akorda. (2019, September 2). *President of Kazakhstan Kassym-Jomart Tokayev's State of the Nation Address*. Akorda. http://www.akorda.kz/en/addresses/addresses_of_president/president-of-kazakhstan-kassymjomart-Tokayevs-state-of-the-nation-address-september-2-2019.

Azernews. (2022, May 10). *Presidential Aide: Heydar Aliyev's Legacy Lives in People's Hearts*. https://www.azernews.az/nation/193579.html

Brownlee, J. (2007). Hereditary Succession in Modern Autocracies. *World Politics, 59*(4), 595–628.

Burkhanov, A., Orazgaliyev, S., & Araral, E. (2021). Political Culture and Power Transition: The Case of Kazakhstan. In J.-F. Caron (Ed.), *Understanding Kazakhstan's 2019 Political Transition* (pp. 7–28). Springer.

Caron, J.-F. (2019a). On the Objectives of Governments: Preventing Domestic Conflicts. In *The Prince 2.0 : Applying Machiavellian Strategy to Contemporary Political Life* (pp. 13–22). Springer.

Caron, J.-F. (2019b). When It Is Necessary to Entrust Governance to One Individual: To Save a Democracy and Its Principles. In *The Prince 2.0 : Applying Machiavellian Strategy to Contemporary Political Life* (pp. 39–44). Springer.

Caron, J.-F., & Malikova, V. (2021). They Stood no Chance : Anti-Regime Activists During the 2019 Kazakhstani Presidential Election. In *Understanding Kazakhstan's 2019 Political Transition* (pp. 79–100). Springer.

Gerschewski, J. (2013). The Three Pillars of Stability: Legitimation, Repression, and Co-optation in Autocratic Regimes. *Democratization, 20*(1), 13–38.

Human Rights Watch. (2019, October 7). *Charting Progress in Mirziyoyev's Uzbekistan*. Human Rights Watch. https://www.hrw.org/news/2019/10/07/charting-progress-mirziyoyevs-uzbekistan.

Isaacs, R. (2013). Nur Otan, Informal Networks and the Countering of Elite Instability in Kazakhstan: Bringing the 'Formal' Back in. *Europe-Asia Studies, 65*(6), 1055–1079.

Junisbai, B. (2010). A Tale of Two Kazakhstans: Sources of Political Cleavage and Conflict in the Post-Soviet Period. *Europe-Asia Studies, 62*(2), 235–269.
Junisbai, B., & Junisbai, A. (2005). Democratic Choice of Kazakhstan: A Case Study in Economic Liberalization, Intra-Elite cleavage, and the Political Opposition. *Demokratizatsiya, 13*(3), 373–392.
Kim, S. P. (1991). Singapore in 1990: Continuity and Stability. *Asian Survey, 31*(2), 172–178.
Kjaenet, H., Satpaev, D., & Torjesen, S. (2008). Big Business and High-Level Politics in Kazakhstan: An Everlasting Symbiosis? *China and Eurasia Quarterly, 6*(1), 631–650.
Lam, P. (1999). Singapore: Rich State; Illiberal Regime. In J. W. Morley (Ed.), *Driven by Growth: Political Change in the Asia-Pacific Region*. M.E. Sharpe.
Lemon, E. (2021). The Kazakh Model? Dynamics of Regime Succession in Eurasia. In J.-F. Caron (Ed.), *Understanding Kazakhstan's 2019 Political Transition* (pp. 53–78). Springer.
Lillis, J. (2018). *Dark Shadows: Inside the Secret World of Kazakhstan*. I.B. Tauris.
McAdam, D., Tarrow, S., & Tilly, C. (2001). *Dynamics of Contention*. Cambridge University Press.
Michel, C. (2015, March 30). Lee Kuan Yew's Singapore as a Model for Kazakhstan. *The Diplomat*. https://thediplomat.com/2015/03/lee-kuan-yews-singapore-as-a-model-for-kazakhstan/
Najibullah, F. (2012, February 13). *Turkmenistan: My Personality Cult Is Better Than Yours*. Radio Free Europe. https://www.rferl.org/a/turkmenistan_berdymukhammedov_cult_of_personality/24482468.html
Pannier, B. (2022, January 12). *The Campaign Against Nazarbaev and the Cronies of Kazakhstan's First President Has Begun*. Radio Free Europe. https://www.rferl.org/a/kazakhstan-nazarbaev-cronies-Tokayev/31651330.html
Reuters. (2019, March 20). In Succession Clue, Kazakh Leader's Daughter Elevated After His Resignation. https://www.reuters.com/article/us-kazakhstan-president-idUSKCN1R10ER
Rodan, G. (1992). Singapore's Leadership Transition: Erosion or Refinement of Authoritarian Rule. *Bulletin of Concerned Asian Scholars, 24*(1), 3–17.
Sattarov, R. (2018, November 16). *Turkmen Leader's Personality Cult Goes Viral*. Carnegie Endowment for International Peace. https://carnegiemoscow.org/commentary/77733
Sorbello, P (2022, December 28). Kazakhstan's Parliament Aims to Take Away Nazarbayev's Privileges. *The Diplomat*. https://thediplomat.com/2022/12/kazakhstans-parliament-aims-to-take-away-nazarbayevs-privileges/
Starr, S. F., & Cornell, S. E. (Eds.). (2018). *Uzbekistan New Face*. Rowman & Littlefield.

Tamura, K. T. (2003). The Emergence and Political Consciousness of the Middle Class in Singapore. *The Developing Economies, 41*(2), 184–200.
Voices of Central Asia. (2017, December 28). *A Year of Economic Reforms with President Mirziyoyev*. Voices of Central Asia. https://voicesoncentralasia.org/a-year-of-economic-reforms-with-president-mirziyoyev/.

Between Threat, Alliance, and Multivectorism: Kazakh-Russian Relations in the Wake of the Russo-Ukrainian War

Thomas Ambrosio

Abstract The January Russian-led, Collective Security Treaty Organization intervention in Kazakhstan on behalf of President Kassym-Jomart Tokayev raised important questions about whether the government in Astana was indebted to Moscow and how much geopolitical leverage the latter could and would exercise over the former. Russia's invasion of Ukraine the following month put Russia-Kazakhstan ties to the test as Kazakhstan has been forced to maneuver through a difficult situation which includes an irredentist threat on its border, a formal alliance with this source of threat, and its official multivector foreign policy. This chapter examines how Kazakhstan has had remarkable success at carefully balancing its deep-rooted ties to Russia with its goal of maintaining both its foreign policy autonomy and positive relations with the West. It also shows how Kazakhstan has taken concrete steps to demonstrate

---

T. Ambrosio (✉)
North Dakota State University, Fargo, ND, USA
e-mail: thomas.ambrosio@ndsu.edu

J.-F. Caron (ed.), *A Revolt in the Steppe*, The Steppe and Beyond: Studies on Central Asia,
https://doi.org/10.1007/978-981-99-0783-0_3

its rejection of Moscow's war aims and to secure its territorial integrity and sovereignty against any potential Russian threat. The conclusion considers what the future might hold for Kazakhstan in light of a dynamic international environment.

Keywords Kazakhstan · Russia · Ukraine · Multivectorism · Irredentism

> *If there is a new iron curtain, we do not want to be behind it.*—Roman Vassilenko, Kazakhstan's Deputy Foreign Minister, March 2022 (Rickleton, 2022)

Russia's invasion of Ukraine in February 2022 not only profoundly impacted Eurasia's geopolitical and security environment, but also it placed Kazakhstan in an especially precarious position. Since 2014, Russia has proven itself to be an irredentist state that may not be satisfied just with territory seized from Ukraine.[1] Because it possesses a substantial ethnic Russian population near the Kazakh-Russian border, Kazakhstan is a potential target of Russian aggression. Moreover, some vocal Russians have questioned Kazakhstan's historical legitimacy, sovereignty, and territorial integrity. However, Kazakhstan remains Russia's formal ally, linked through a dense web of bilateral and multilateral security, economic, and political ties from which Astana would find itself nearly impossible to untangle. As such, Kazakhstan is effectively locked into a close relationship with a source of potential and significant threat. At the same time, Kazakhstan also aspires to implement a "multivector" foreign policy, through which it hopes to maintain positive relations with various centers of geopolitical power. Prior to February 2022, this strategy was already showing strains resulting from worsening relations between Russia and the West. These strains have only intensified because of Russia's pariah status in Western capitals. Complicating all of this are the events of January 2022 when Russia led an intervention by the Collective Security Treaty Organization (CSTO) on behalf of Kazakh President Kassym-Jomart Tokayev in January 2022 when widespread, violent protests threatened his rule. This raised questions about whether

[1] And possibly, Georgia, depending on whether South Ossetia votes to join the Russian Federation.

the already-unequal relationship between Moscow and Astana would tilt in the former's direction and whether this could be used as leverage over Tokayev's government.

This chapter examines Kazakhstan's foreign and domestic policies in the wake of the Russo-Ukrainian War as it seeks to maneuver through a difficult situation which blends threat, alliance, multivectorism, and dependence. It demonstrates that the conventional wisdom regarding Russia's future influence over Kazakhstan after the January 2022 intervention has been proven wrong. Instead, Astana has had remarkable success in carefully balancing its deep-rooted ties to Moscow with its goal of maintaining both its foreign policy autonomy and positive relations with the West. It has also taken steps to secure its territorial integrity and sovereignty against any potential Russian threat.

The longer the war persists, however, Kazakhstan's policy dexterity may be put in jeopardy as chances increase of a descent of a new iron curtain of the sort which Vassilenko fears. The country may yet have to make a fateful choice. At the very least, the danger of a revanchist Russia will continue to loom over the region.

This chapter begins with a broad overview of Kazakhstan's strategic environment prior to 2022. It then discusses the circumstances surrounding the January 2022 intervention and questions raised at the time regarding future Kazakh-Russian relations. The following sections examine different aspects of Kazakhstan's response to the Russo-Ukrainian War: how Kazakhstan has sought to distance itself from Russia's war internationally; how it has undertaken symbolic and practical steps domestically against a possible Russian threat; and, the persistence of the country's close ties with Russia despite intensified rhetorical threats against the country and the ongoing economic costs associated with the war. The conclusion considers what the future might hold for Kazakhstan in light of a dynamic international environment.

Pre-2022 Strategic Environment

Kazakhstan's strategic situation was already complicated prior to 2022. Since independence, its foreign policy had been guided by the principle of "multivectorism," which actively sought to maintain positive relations with the major power centers which intersected in Central Asia: Russia, the West, China, and the Islamic world. This was to be achieved through extensive bilateral and multilateral relations with each "vector," avoiding conflicts within and between them, and not fully committing to any specific direction. Kazakhstan's founding leader, President Nursultan Nazarbayev, framed multivectorism as necessary to secure his country's sovereignty and independence by ensuring that it and the wider Central Asian region was not pulled into "an unpredictable vortex of various regional conflicts of military, political, economic, and confessional nature"—an outcome which was more likely to occur if the "bloc and alliance" mentalities of the past were to recur (Nazarbayev, 1997). When necessary, Kazakhstan sought to play the roles of mediator and bridge between opposing parties (Ambrosio & Lange, 2015, 551).

Multivectorism has been successful in the main, but has been undercut by two factors. First, Sullivan (2019) described how Astana has had to shift from "proactive" to "reactive" multivectorism as relations between Russia and the West deteriorated during Russian President Vladimir Putin's second term. Proactive multivectorism was the ideal foreign policy concept outlined by Nazarbayev in the 1990s. It was something which could be positively asserted to actively improve Kazakhstan's geopolitical circumstances and was easier to achieve when the various vectors had at least neutral relations with each other. By contrast, reactive multilateralism represented a form of damage control which is focused on mitigating the harms associated with trying to maintain good relations with conflicting actors. In particular, it was meant to compensate for the way in which Russian interventions in Georgia in 2008, Ukraine in 2014, and Syria in 2015 harmed relations between Russia and the West and how Kazakhstan increasingly found itself in the middle of this renewed east-west conflict—the precise bloc and alliance mentality feared by Nazarbayev. Caught in this dilemma, Kazakhstan sought to have it both ways: not openly backing Russia's actions out of fear of damaging relations with the West, despite the Kremlin's calls for such support, but also not openly opposing Russian actions for fear of angering Moscow, even though Kazakhstan found Russia's interventions troubling. The challenges associated with navigating this middle ground were already worsening by the end of 2021.

Second, Kazakhstan never actually adhered to a truly multivector foreign policy. It has certainly been able to maintain positive relations and active cooperation with states with a variety of opposing interests. This should not be discounted. However, the pattern since independence has been a steady institutional alignment toward Russia without comparable or offsetting alignments toward the other vectors (Ambrosio,

2021). This is seen most clearly in Kazakhstan's membership in the Russian-dominated Eurasian Economic Union (EAEU) and the Collective Security Treaty Organization (CSTO), as well as the disproportionate number of bilateral agreements with Russia in the economic and security realms. The EAEU is an economic bloc modeled upon the European Union (EU) and aims to integrate the economies of several former Soviet Union (FSU) states. Although its members are not restricted from trading with non-EAEU states, it has effectively institutionalized Russia's outsized economic influence over the region. The CSTO is a military alliance with mutual security guarantees and is far more exclusionary. Not only are members prohibited from joining an alternative military alliance, but a non-binding (but controlling) decision by the CSTO governing council also prohibits non-member military bases within CSTO space without unanimous consent—effectively giving Moscow a veto. Moreover, Russia has utilized the organization to legitimize its military presence throughout the FSU and the alliance's emphasis on interoperability has meant that its members remain dependent on Russian military equipment and training. It thus ensures that Moscow remains the FSU's dominant security actor. Although neither the EAEU nor the CSTO have truly lived up to their potential—or their public marketing—both have effectively oriented their members toward Moscow through interlocking and reinforcing institutions.

Kazakhstan's unbalanced orientation toward Russia makes sense given their long border and extensive historical, cultural, economic, and security connections, but is also a potential source of threat as Russia could exploit these ties to gain leverage over the country. This is compounded by the demographic reality of Kazakhstan being home to a substantial, albeit declining, ethnic Russian population in the country's northern provinces. Following Russia's annexation of Crimea in 2014, the prospect of further Russian irredentism became very real with Kazakhstan seen as a particularly vulnerable target. In 2014, Putin made comments which seemingly called into question Kazakhstan's pre-1991 nationhood (Najibullah, 2014)—comments which paralleled those made against Ukraine. These were seconded by politicians in Russia and among some ethnic Russians in Kazakhstan itself (Michel, 2022; Pannier, 2022; Shapoo, 2022), raising concerns about whether Moscow might one day enact a "Ukraine scenario" in Kazakhstan (de Haas, 2017, pp. 631, 642). Kazakhstan took this threat seriously, as evidenced by significant changes to its post-2014 national security documents (Ambrosio, 2022). These revised documents now emphasized the dangers of separatism and the hybrid warfare techniques Russian forces used in Crimea and were supplemented by various policies to reinforce Kazakhstan's national identity, sovereignty, and territorial integrity. Although Russia was not specifically named as their cause, their timing and specifics left little room for doubt as the threat from Russia was seen as being very real. Nonetheless, upon succeeding Nazarbayev, President Tokayev consistently reaffirmed the Russia-Kazakhstan alliance and his new government took no steps to disentangle itself from Russia (Ambrosio, 2021). This created a situation in which Kazakhstan remained institutionally linked to a source of threat.

Each of the forces which shaped Kazakhstan's broader security environment prior to 2022—a strained multivector foreign policy, Astana's deep and extensive ties with Moscow, and the very real threat posed by Russia—was magnified by Russia's aggression against Ukraine in February 2022. However, before Kazakhstan's government had to confront this problem, it faced a threat to its very survival.

CSTO Intervention

On 2 January 2022, protests began in the western city of Zhanaozen following the removal of price controls on fuel (International Crisis Group, 2022; Siheon Nathaniel Choi et al., 2022). Although the demonstrations appeared spontaneous and no leaders emerged to guide them, they rapidly spread across the country. Opposition to price increases soon transitioned into calls for substantial political and economic reforms and, for some protestors, the complete removal of the government. By 5 January, several government buildings in Almaty were occupied and some were set ablaze. Scores of protesters and law enforcement officers were killed in clashes. This led President Tokayev to formally request CSTO intervention to combat the "terrorist gangs" who were "trained abroad" and allegedly in league with some members of Kazakhstan's security services (Meduza, 2022). Within hours, Russian paratroopers were deployed and shortly followed by smaller contingents from other CSTO members. This was the first CSTO intervention on behalf of a member country and therefore was a sharp departure from previous situations in which the alliance refused to act despite similar requests, such as in Kyrgyzstan in 2005, 2010, and 2020, Armenia in 2020, and Tajikistan in 2021 (Ruehl, 2022).

CSTO forces took no part in forcefully putting down the protests, but rather secured strategic locations around Kazakhstan to free up the government's loyal security services to focus on restoring order (Choi et al., 2022; Simes, 2022). The estimated number of CSTO troops sent into Kazakhstan ranged widely between 2,500 and 4,000, with the vast majority—at least three-quarters—coming from Russia, which directed the operation (Beliakova, 2022; Hedenskog & von Essen, 2022). A week later they departed.

There are many questions surrounding the uprising and the CSTO operation. Were the protests used as cover for a behind-the-scenes intra-elite struggle between supporters of the current President and his predecessor, who maintained significant power and might have been angling to put his daughter in the presidency? To what degree were Kazakhstan's security forces compromised? Why did the CSTO intervene here when it had refused to do so before? Had the CSTO not intervened, was Tokayev's government ever in serious danger of falling? The answers to these questions are either unanswerable without insider information or unprovable counterfactuals. It is possible, however, to consider some of the operation's implications.

Not only was the CSTO intervention unprecedented and signified the organization's transition from a passive to an active actor within the FSU, but more importantly it made plain that Russia was the dominant security actor within the region in terms of both state and now *regime* security, as it was now willing and able to intervene militarily to preserve the political status quo within its allies. Moscow already demonstrated this in Belarus in 2020, when Russian security personnel (without the help of other CSTO forces) helped President Alexander Lukashenko resist a widespread post-election uprising which nearly toppled his regime. Tokayev's survival confirmed that Russia was also able to employ the CSTO as a multilateral means to "deter coups, prevent security forces' defections, and limit the success of popular protests in Russia's sphere of influence" (Beliakova, 2022). At a CSTO summit held on 10 January, President Putin summarized the alliance's new role as such: a "colour revolution" would no longer be allowed to take place within "our states"—a statement which should probably be read as Russia not being willing to allow this within what it sees as *its* region ("Session of CSTO…", 2022).

Even if Tokayev's political survival was not actually in danger, his request to the CSTO clearly indicated that he perceived that it was and that he needed Russia to shore up his regime. The symbolism of Russia seemingly coming to his rescue raised considerable questions about the degree to which Tokayev's government was now dependent on Moscow. How much more influence would Russia have over Kazakhstan? Did this represent a form of political debt which Astana would have to pay off in the future? Under what circumstances could and would the Kremlin leverage this to direct Kazakhstan's domestic and foreign policies? These questions took on vital importance the following month when the Kremlin precipitated the greatest geopolitical upheaval of the post-Soviet space—and within Europe as a whole—since the collapse of the USSR.

Setting the Stage

Kazakhstan's strategic predicament prior to 2022 consisted of being aligned with a potential source of threat which it would not or could not disengage from, but also seeking to maintain a degree of foreign policy multilateralism in an international system progressively defined by zero-sum conflict between Russia and the West. This sharply intensified following Russia's invasion of Ukraine in February 2022. Russia had already shown contempt for its neighbors' territorial integrity in the recent past, as seen in Georgia in 2008, Crimea in 2014, and through its continual support for separatists in eastern Ukraine. Russia's invasion of Ukraine was profoundly different, as any pretense that Russia would be satisfied with being a benevolent regional power was blatantly, and violently, discredited. Its potential impact for Kazakhstan was best summarized by a sign held by one anti-war protestor in the country: "Вчера Грузия. Сегодня Украина. А завтра Казахстан?"—"Yesterday, Georgia. Today, Ukraine. And tomorrow, Kazakhstan?" (Prokhvatilov, 2022). The question for Kazakhstan was how to respond.

Despite its close ties with Russia, Kazakhstan has displayed a remarkable willingness to distance itself from Russian aggression, take actions domestically to secure its sovereignty and independence, refuse to assist Russia in avoiding sanctions, and maintain positive relations with Western countries. Assumptions about any quid-pro-quo between Putin and Tokayev for future support have proven to be incorrect. Nonetheless, Kazakhstan remains aligned with Russia despite hostile rhetoric exhibited by some prominent Russians, the increasing economic spillover associated with the war and Western sanctions, and the potential reputational costs of being associated with a country which the West considers an aggressor.

The absence of any indication that Kazakhstan seeks to undertake a fundamental rethinking of its relationship with Moscow indicates that Astana realizes that its strategic options are limited.

Distancing Kazakhstan Internationally

According to Timur Suleimenov, the first deputy chief of staff to the President of Kazakhstan, "of course, Russia wanted us to be more on their side" in Ukraine, but "we don't want and will not risk being placed in the same basket" as Russia (Gotev, 2022). To this end, Kazakhstan claimed that it is a neutral party in the war, neither condoning nor openly criticizing Russia's invasion. This sentiment was best expressed by Deputy Defense Minister Sultan Kamaletdinov who said, "the conflict between Russia and Ukraine has nothing to do with Kazakhstan. We do not support either side" (Waal, 2022).

Kamaletdinov's claim has proven to be not fully accurate. On balance, Kazakhstan has opposed Russia's core war aims, setting itself in de facto opposition to its ally. For example, Astana has not followed Moscow's lead in recognizing the independence of the Donetsk and Luhansk Republics, a position reiterated in June at a joint press conference between Tokayev and Putin in which Tokayev made clear his support for state sovereignty over self-determination ("Kazakhstan's President Addresses…", 2022). Kazakhstan also refused to recognize Russia's September annexation of Ukraine's Donetsk, Kherson, Luhansk, and Zaporizhzhia oblasts on the grounds that it "views this issue from the perspective of the territorial integrity of the state" ("Kazakhstan MFA about…", 2022). These actions were consistent with its earlier refusal to recognize the independence of South Ossetia and Abkhazia, as well as the legality of Russia's annexation of Crimea. Instead, Kazakh officials have made several statements supportive of Ukraine's territorial integrity within its post-independence borders and affirmed that it would maintain positive relations with Ukraine, regardless of the state of war between Moscow and Kyiv.[2] Furthermore, Kazakhstan abstained from two March 2022 United Nations General Assembly resolutions which characterized Russia's actions as aggression. Granted, it did not vote in favor of the resolutions, as did the majority of the UN's members. However, it was

[2] The most prominent of which was Tokayev's (2022) article in *The National Interest*.

perhaps telling that Kazakhstan neither voted against them, like Belarus, nor was it conveniently absent from the votes, like some other FSU countries. Its abstentions should therefore be taken as a willingness to show its unease about Russia's actions, but without going too far.

Kazakhstan also made clear that it would neither help Russia evade Western sanctions nor would it allow the EAEU to do so (Kumenov, 2022e). This was significant since Kazakhstan could easily have served as an effective conduit for the transit of prohibited goods. Instead, it restricted access of sanctioned Russian corporations from doing business in Kazakhstan and barred its own corporations from doing business with sanctioned individuals and businesses. In addition, despite an earlier pledge to eventually shift toward a single ruble zone and a request from Moscow to now use rubles for the collection of customs duties, Kazakhstan refused, maintaining that payments remain in US dollars (Stronski, 2022). Thus, Kazakhstan did little to ease the economic fallout from Russia's war.

This, like reactive multivectorism more generally, was ultimately reflective of a strategy of damage control. During a late-March visit to Brussels for discussions with EU officials, Suleimenov explicitly stated that Kazakhstan sought to avoid "secondary sanctions of the US and the EU" by "demonstrat[ing] to our European partners that Kazakhstan will not be a tool to circumvent the sanctions on Russia by the US and the EU" (Gotev, 2022). In addition, he asked them for forbearance, given that Kazakhstan remains a member of the EAEU and will, therefore, remain closely tied to Russia economically for the foreseeable future. Because of this, Kazakh officials noted that Kazakhstan's businesses will be allowed to continue to invest in Russia, as well as to accept investments from Russia. Nonetheless, it promised vigilance against sanctions violations—a compromise which the EU accepted.

Kazakhstan's outreach to the West was not just defensive, however. Kazakh officials also expressed their desire to positively enhance cooperation with the West, despite the possible negative reaction from Russia. While this would bring economic benefits in the form of increased trade and further foreign investment, it was also intended to ensure that Kazakhstan was able to maintain diversity in its diplomatic and economic relations. It is perhaps telling that this desire to strengthen relations with the West also included a concerted effort to reinforce Kazakhstan's "enhanced strategic partnership" with the United States, as Mukhtar Tileuberdi, Deputy Prime Minister and Minister of Foreign Affairs, said during an April visit to Washington ("On the Talks...", 2022).[3] The fact that Tileuberdi was still willing to use this language in relation to a country that is engaged in an open proxy war against Russia is illustrative of the degree to which Astana felt the need to pursue an independent foreign policy, even if that seemed at odds with its close relationship with Moscow.

Domestic Responses to the War

Kazakhstan also took symbolic and concrete steps at home to reflect its concern over Russia's invasion of Ukraine. For example, authorities granted a permit to activists to hold a demonstration in Almaty on 6 March. Although this was technically a general anti-war protest, it was very clearly anti-Russian and pro-Ukrainian, replete with Ukrainian flags and signs calling out Russian aggression (Lillis & Imanaliyeva, 2022; Rickleton, 2022). It was noteworthy that it was even allowed to occur at all, coming just two months after the January violence which had so vividly illustrated how protests could assume a life of their own. Despite the potential risk to the government, it seemingly wanted to send a signal to Moscow—one which was reinforced by the fact that no pro-Russian demonstrations were allowed to occur. Additionally, the government permitted some low-level, but surprisingly open, discussion regarding Kazakhstan's alignment with Russia, including questions about its membership in the EAEU and CSTO (Marat & Engvall, 2022; Nurgozhayeva, 2022). Although the government itself remained steadfast in its commitment toward maintaining its close relationship with Russia through these organizations, allowing these discussions to occur within the public space was a departure for a regime which has often suppressed deviations from the government's foreign policy line. Kazakhstan also allowed its citizens to collect humanitarian aid for Ukraine and supplemented this with its own donations (Lillis & Imanaliyeva, 2022; Volkmann-Schluck, 2022).

Kazakhstan also canceled its public 2022 Victory Day celebrations, marking the holiday instead with either low-key or online ceremonies (Altynbayev, 2022b; "Kazakhstan marks Victory Day", 2022). Beginning under the Soviet Union, Victory Day was meant to mark the Soviet

[3] Also see Satubaldina (2022).

Union's defeat of Nazi Germany—a tradition which was continued by some of the post-Soviet states, including Kazakhstan. More recently, however, Victory Day became a centerpiece of the Kremlin's post-Soviet national identity-building efforts and an event which it has used to stoke Russian nationalism and anti-Western sentiments. Although Kazakhstan failed to hold Victory Day parades every year since independence, it did hold them occasionally, and most recently in 2018. In 2019, then-President Nazarbayev traveled to Moscow to celebrate the holiday with Putin ("Nursultan Nazarbayev attended…", 2019). Public events were cancelled in 2020 and 2021 because of the COVID-19 pandemic. With the pandemic's wane, Kazakhstan was set to revive the tradition, including a military parade, fireworks, school activities, and a procession by those who lost family during World War II (Altynbayev, 2022b). Although Kazakhstan's government did not directly tie its cancelation to concerns over the war—blaming it instead on budgetary and "other issues"—the implication appeared to be clear: Astana did not want to be seen as holding parallel celebrations along with Russia while Moscow was engaged in a war of aggression against Ukraine (Sánchez & Auyezova, 2022).

Kazakhstan also permitted upward of 300,000 Russians fleeing the Kremlin's September conscription order to enter the country. Tokayev openly showed sympathy toward their plight, declaring that "most of them are forced to leave because of the current hopeless situation" and that his government "must take care of them and ensure their safety" (Askar, 2022). Moreover, the government stated that it would neither deport nor extradite those fleeing without an international arrest warrant. In fact, many of them would be permitted to apply for an "individual identification number," which would allow them to live and work in the country for the medium-term. Rather than helping its ally replenish its already-depleted pool of military-age personnel, Kazakhstan, in effect, allowed Russia's predicament to worsen.

Astana also took more concrete actions to secure its sovereignty and territorial integrity. For example, Kazakhstan's television providers dropped some Kremlin-controlled broadcasting from the country almost immediately after the invasion (Altynbayev, 2022a; "Russian Journalists Accuse…", 2022). In Ukraine, as well as elsewhere, Russian media has been accused of a means by which Moscow could exert soft power and promote disinformation, nationalism, and ethnic division. While the government did not take responsibility for this move, its timing was more than just a bit conspicuous and reflected fears about how Russian propaganda might seek to stir Kazakhstan's ethnic Russian population or, more generally, persuade Kazakh citizens to pressure their government to support Russia's war. These fears were made explicit by a directive from Kazakhstan's Prosecutor's Office issued the following month which warned that "materials related to the conflict between the Russian Federation and Ukraine" could lead to the "destabilization of [Kazakhstan's] socio-political situation" ("Deputy Prosecutor General...", 2022). In this document, the government reminded its citizens that "separatist appeals," publicly questioning Kazakhstan's territorial integrity, inciting ethnic hatred, or disseminating "knowingly false information" were all illegal and could lead to imprisonment. Moreover, the government began de facto restrictions on open displays of pro-Russian symbols, especially the now-infamous "Z" letter which came to represent support for Russia's military operation (Stronski, 2022). The government also initiated an investigation into a social media post in which a media personality suggested that ethnic Russians in Kazakhstan might call upon Russia to intervene on their behalf (Kumenov, 2022c). In August, a couple were each sentenced to five years in prison for a social media conversation in which they called for northern Kazakhstan to become part of Russia ("Kazakh Court Sentences...", 2022). Even statements made outside of Kazakhstan came under scrutiny, as the government threatened to bar individuals from entering the country if they used similar language (Agence France-Presse, 2022).

This sense of threat was also reflected in Kazakhstan's security policy. It is likely not a coincidence that Kazakh officials placed the country's military on high alert and repositioned its forces throughout the country in late February (Kumenov, 2022d). While the government claimed that this was all just part of a pre-planned military exercise ("The Movement of Military...", 2022), this is difficult to believe given its timing and as this explanation came after the fact. More importantly, a significant increase in Kazakhstan's military spending was announced in April despite Kazakhstan's declining economic prospects which was already putting pressure on its budget (Kumenov, 2022d). Nonetheless, the government felt the need to spend more on its defense.

The government also released proposed changes to Kazakhstan's 2017 military doctrine which included a new emphasis on the threat from the "hidden preparation of destructive elements on the territory of the Republic of Kazakhstan and neighboring states" ("On Amendments to…", 2022). This clause did not make it into the final version ("On Amendments and…", 2022), but the emphasis on preventing separatism remained. More importantly, multivectorism was now enshrined in the updated doctrine as being critical for ensuring Kazakhstan's national security. Although this was consistent with the country's post-independence foreign policy, its inclusion here at this time should likely be taken as a signal to Moscow that was keeping its options open. Moreover, a reference to participating in joint exercises with NATO, which was present in the 2017 military doctrine, was not dropped despite the open confrontation between Russia and the alliance over Ukraine. This, too, was likely intended to be a signal to Moscow that Russia's enemies were not Kazakhstan's.

Certainly, some of these security steps were caused by the unprecedented domestic violence associated with the January protests and not everything should be seen as a consequence of the war (Gleason, 2022). However, the renewed threat from Russian irredentism almost certainly contributed to them.

Continuing Dominance of the Russian "Vector"

While these international and domestic actions are evidence of Kazakhstan's deep concern over Russia's invasion of Ukraine, it is also apparent that Kazakhstan will not, and likely cannot, fundamentally reorient itself away from Russia. Despite intensified rhetorical threats emanating from inside Russia and ongoing costs associated with remaining so closely tied to its northern neighbor economically, the Russian "vector" continues to dominate Kazakhstan's economic and security policies.

Intensified Rhetorical Threats from Russia

It is important to note that Kazakhstan's post-February 2022 actions persisted even in the face of some prominent Russian commentators, journalists, and politicians who attacked Nur-Sultan for not fully backing Moscow's war in Ukraine. These critics called it a betrayal and threatening Kazakhstan with similar treatment if it did not reverse its stance. Emblematic of this is the statement by Tigran Keosayan, the husband of the editor-in-chief of Kremlin-controlled *Russia Today* and *Rossiya Segodnya* who, in response to Astana's cancelation of Victory Day celebrations, warned Kazakhs to "look at Ukraine carefully, think seriously

(Putz, 2022b)."[4] In some cases, the rhetoric used against Kazakhstan has been eerily similar to that used against Ukraine, such as calling it full of "little Nazis"—a phrase which directly mirrored the Kremlin's claims that it is undertaking a "denazification" campaign in Ukraine (Globe, 2022).[5] The insinuation being, of course, that Russia might have to denazify Kazakhstan as well. Others made more direct territorial claims, such as Konstantin Zatulin, first deputy chairman of State Duma committee dealing with the former USSR and ethnic Russians abroad, who noted during an interview with *Radio Moskva* that "there are many towns with a predominantly Russian population that have little to do with what was called Kazakhstan" (Lautman, 2022). According to Zatulin, while Russia would not act on this while Kazakhstan was still a friend and a partner, that could change, as it had with Ukraine. Although the Kremlin itself has not adopted this language and Kazakhstan's relations with Russia since independence have been far better than Kyiv had with Moscow, the fact that these rhetorical attacks are occurring so publicly is troubling.

Economic Costs of the Russo-Ukrainian War

Because the two economies are so intertwined, the Russo-Ukrainian War has negatively impacted Kazakhstan. Eighty percent of Kazakhstan's oil exports and fifty percent of its overall trade transit through Russian territory (Umarov, 2022). This has caused "many problems to many industries in Kazakhstan," according to Suleimenov (Gotev, 2022). Although the search for alternative export routes started immediately after the invasion, Kazakhstan's industries and the state budget have already been hurt (Volkmann-Schluck, 2022). For example, the primary pipeline that exports Kazakhstan's oil was repeatedly restricted or shut down altogether by Russia since the war began ("Russia Reverses Course...", 2022). While it is important not be "reductionist" and see all such events as part of a geopolitical "energy weapon" conspiracy by the Kremlin (Judge et al., 2016, 755), some of these have occurred under questionable circumstances. One occurred just a days after Tokayev participated in the Kremlin's showcase International Economic Forum in mid-June, in which he reaffirmed that Kazakhstan supported Ukraine's territorial

[4] Also see "Russian Journalists Accuse..." (2022).

[5] Also see Tazhutov (2022) and Bezpalko (2022).

integrity and would respect Western sanctions against Russia while he was (Lautman, 2022). Russia claimed that this shutdown was due to the sudden discovery of unexploded World War II munitions near a critical pipeline terminal. Oil flows resumed shortly thereafter, only to be cut off again by a Russian court which ruled that "irregularities in paperwork guiding elimination of oil spill emergencies" required a thirty-day suspension of operations (Lautman, 2022). This ruling occurred the day after Tokayev stated that his country would seek to assist the EU in meeting its energy needs associated with disruptions of imports from Russia—a policy which would have the effect of undermining Moscow's energy leverage over Europe (Abbasova, 2022). While this was changed to an extremely small fine a few days later, it was yet another reminder of Kazakhstan's dependence upon Russia for its economic well-being. The Kazakhstan government is seeking alternative pipelines—most notably through Azerbaijan—but these cannot replace the Russian transit routes in the short term.

Additional economic impacts of the war include the costs incurred by Kazakh manufacturers having to shift export routes away from Russia out of an abundance of caution, so as to avoid being accused of helping Russia avoid sanctions, as well as because some Western countries have simply refused to accept products which have transited Russian territory (Kumenov, 2022b). Sanctions against Russia have also had damaging effects on Kazakhstan's economy in other ways. The overall slowdown in the Russian economy hurt Kazakhstan's manufacturers exporting to Russia as ordinary Russians tighten their belts. Moreover, Kazakhstan's inflation rate jumped significantly once the war began and continued to rise six months later as a result of the initial, post-invasion drop in Kazakhstan's national currency because of its connections to the ruble, the drop in global wheat production brought on by restricted Ukrainian and Russian exports, and a temporary ban on the export of foodstuffs imposed by Moscow ("Kazakhstan Inflation Rate" 2022). In response, Kazakhstan has had to restrict its own exports of wheat and wheat flour, which were becoming increasingly profitable prior to the war (Kumenov, 2022a). There were also concerns that Russian exporters will seek to unload their now-unexportable products at a discount within the EAEU economic space in order to recoup some revenues, thus harming Kazakhstan's domestic industries (Volkmann-Schluck, 2022). Finally, although Kazakhstan does not rely as much on remittances from Russia as many of its fellow Central Asian countries, the economic downturn in Russia and the return of now-unemployed Kazakh workers will still have an effect (Putz, 2022a).

Given that the January protests were sparked by socioeconomic issues, Kazakhstan's close economic ties to Russia creates a potentially dangerous situation for Tokayev's government. However, well-established and extensive trading relationships are hard to change in the short term without severe negative consequences. Russia is Kazakhstan's second-largest trading partner and, as Tokayev noted, trade between the two countries has increased almost a third in 2021, making Russia "Kazakhstan's key economic partner in the EAEU" ("St Petersburg International..., 2022)." Rather than pulling away, Kazakhstan reaffirmed its commitment to the EAEU and the broader Eurasian integration project, despite some on Kazakh social media claiming that it should (and, indeed, was planning to) leave the organization ("Kazakhstan has No...", 2022). While the current situation has caused the government to redouble its efforts to diversify its economic connections outside of the EAEU ("Expansion of Partnership...", 2022), the economies of Kazakhstan and Russia remain inexorably linked.

Security Ties

Kazakhstan also remains bound to Russia in the security sphere, despite the potential threat that Russia poses. During a May 2022 summit marking the thirtieth anniversary of the Collective Security Treaty, Tokayev spoke of the alliance's "serious potential for further development" and called for it to take on a new role in international peacekeeping operations ("CSTO Summit" 2022). While the CSTO did not support Russia's military operation diplomatically—which Lukashenko demanded that it do during the summit—the statement issued by the heads of state reaffirmed the members' commitment to the alliance ("Statement by the Collective...", 2022). Furthermore, references to the CSTO remained in Kazakhstan's draft military doctrine and the country hosted a series of alliance military exercises in October 2022 ("The Republic of Kazakhstan...", 2022). Although the alliance's intervention in the January unrest clearly did not put Astana in Moscow's debt, it has revitalized the organization, likely giving it new purpose.[6]

Furthermore, following his reelection in November 2022, Tokayev's first foreign visit was to Russia which, he admitted "has political significance and, of course, a certain symbolism" ("Kazakhstan's Toqaev Tells...", 2022). During his meeting with Putin, Tokayev commented that, "for Kazakhstan, Russia is and always has been a strategic partner." In addition, the two Presidents signed a declaration commemorating thirty years of diplomatic relations between the two states and reaffirmed their commitment to a series of foundational treaties which, according to Putz (2022d) , "form the bedrock of their close relationship." In short, Astana's overarching strategic orientation toward Moscow persists despite disagreements over the war in Ukraine.

Conclusion

The fears expressed in the opening of this chapter have not come to pass. An iron curtain has not fallen over the world because of Russia's invasion of Ukraine. Instead, many countries have been able to maintain positive relations with Moscow without calling into question their relationship with the West. Fortunately, Kazakhstan has not had to make a choice between the two. However, the war is still unfolding as of this writing and, should things qualitatively escalate, Astana's balancing act may become unfeasible. While the situation remains highly volatile, some preliminary conclusions can be reached.

The Tokayev government has proven that it is not indebted to the Kremlin for the Russian-led, CSTO intervention in January 2022. In contrast to his statements during a visit to Russia the following month, in which Tokayev was rather effusive about the CSTO's role in helping his government restore order ("Meeting with President...", 2022), his later comments downplayed its impact (Putz, 2022c). Whether the intervention was instrumental in keeping Tokayev in power is beside the point for purposes of this chapter. Instead, what is important is that Kazakhstan is clearly not following Russia's lead on the war regardless of what occurred in January. It has taken steps at home and abroad to distance

[6] This may be temporary, however, given that the CSTO did not intervene on Armenia' behalf in September 2022 when Yerevan formally invoked the alliance's mutual defense clause in response to what it claimed was Azerbaijani aggression.

itself symbolically and concretely from Russian actions, to maintain and even strengthen ties with Russia's foes, and to respond to the perceived deterioration in its threat environment. In sharp contrast to Russia's de facto suzerainty over Belarus, Kazakhstan's foreign and domestic policies have deftly preserved the country's autonomy and independence.

Nonetheless, there is no indication—at least one which is public—that the government is considering a fundamental change in the country's primary economic or security orientation toward Russia. Kazakhstan is seemingly not even able to go as far as to condemn Russia's invasion of Ukraine as an act of aggression and a violation of international law, calling it instead a "challenging" situation and a "tragedy" (Tokayev 2022). This reflects Kazakhstan's geopolitical realities. The country is inescapably tied to Russia by history, geography, and demographics, reinforced by a dense web of post-Soviet economic and security commitments at the bilateral and multilateral levels. This means that even if Astana truly sought such a reorientation, it would be, at best, extremely difficult to achieve. At worst, Moscow could react sharply, especially if this were attempted in the security realm. Kazakhstan's close, positive working relationship with Russia is a matter of necessity, even if Moscow has now proven itself to be an aggressive irredentist state and, therefore, a real and present danger. Simply put, Kazakhstan has no alternative.

Kazakhstan's success in navigating these fraught waters has been facilitated by several factors. First, beyond Belarus and a few other states, no other country has fully backed Russia, even within the FSU. Despite repeated requests by Moscow to do so, even China has been unwilling to openly support its geopolitical and strategic partner out of fear of Western sanctions (Cadell & Nakashima, 2022). This provides Kazakhstan with a cache of diplomatic cover to distance itself from Russia. Second, Kazakhstan has been successfully able to frame its international actions as an extension of its long-standing policy of multivectorism, rather than recent disloyalty born from fear or opportunism. Third, Russia's military difficulties in Ukraine mean that Moscow needs all the friends that it can get and it has little choice other than to accept Kazakhstan's ambivalence. Thus, even though Astana has made overtures toward Russia's geopolitical enemies, any potential backlash from Moscow has been mitigated. Lastly, the West evidently recognizes Kazakhstan's geopolitical quandary and has responded positively to Kazakhstan's attempts to strike a geopolitical balance. Some in the United States reportedly see the current situation an opportunity to drive a wedge between Astana and Moscow which may come to fruition sometime in the future (Bhadrakumar, 2022). For the time being, the West seems to be content to rely on carrots to one day entice it away from Russia, rather than forcing it choose between them through sticks. In short, conditions are such that Kazakhstan has been able to pay minimal diplomatic costs for its post-invasion foreign policy.

These conditions are subject to change, of course, depending upon the outcome of the war. Russia may well emerge from the conflict considerably weakened. Even if speculation of the Russian Federation going the way of the Soviet Union seems hyperbolic, it will take some time for Russia to rebuild its hard and soft power. This will leave Kazakhstan and the other FSU states in a stronger position vis-à-vis Russia, likely providing them with greater leverage in the relationship. At the extreme end, this may even open an opportunity for them to move away from Moscow without fearing any negative consequences.

On the other hand, it is just as likely that Russia will succeed in Ukraine in some substantive way. Russia will still have to rebuild, certainly, but the FSU states may find themselves confronted with a reinvigorated hegemon that has once again demonstrated that it is willing and able to impose its will in the region, even at great cost to itself. These fears were embodied in a long post published on the *Vkontakte* account of former Russian President (and current deputy chair of the Russian Security Council) Dmitry Medvedev, in which he reportedly called Kazakhstan an "artificial state" and that its lands were rightfully Russia's (Sorbello, 2022). The post was quickly taken down and Medvedev's spokespeople claimed that his account was hacked. Nonetheless, Medvedev regularly makes hawkish statements and, even if disavowed, the post brought renewed focus on the fact that Kazakhstan's situation remains dangerous. Given the country's geographic and demographic circumstances, any rebalancing in Russia's favor will impact Kazakhstan disproportionately.

If the war were to drag on for some time, not only would the economic costs for the world, generally, and for Kazakhstan, specifically, continue to pile up, but Kazakhstan's multivector foreign policy may become less tenable over time. What we see now is a mixture of reactive multivectorism—neither supporting nor opposing Russian actions—and attempts to return to more active multivectorism, as evidenced by its overtures toward the West. How long will the West allow Kazakhstan to maintain its close relationship with Russia without paying any price? Kazakhstan has been careful about not violating the West's sanctions and the status quo may be allowed to go for the foreseeable future. However, the West's attitude toward Russia's allies may harden, not necessarily out of a desire to punish Russia's allies, but rather in an attempt to further isolate Moscow. Kazakhstan may one day be forced to make a choice that it desperate seeks to avoid.

Finally, the Russo-Ukrainian War will undoubtedly increase China's influence and role in Central Asia. The pattern to date has been one in which Beijing sees the region primarily through the lens of economics. To this end, it has openly respected Russia's dominant security role there so as not to appear to threaten Russia's interests and to avoid precipitating a negative reaction by Moscow. However, Central Asia is not only a place where China is now heavily invested, but it also serves as a critical hub in China's Belt and Road Initiative. While the arrangement between the two great powers appears stable, Beijing's interests in Central Asia are only growing and it has already been more willing to greater involve itself in the region's political and security issues (Šćepanović, 2022). Might China seek to leverage its growing influence and Russia's current weakness to its advantage? If so, then Kazakhstan may find itself pulled in three, rather than two directions.

Kazakhstan's predicament prior to the Russo-Ukrainian War—aligned with a potential source of threat from which it will not or cannot extricate itself—has only intensified since February 2022. Thus far, the country has been able to successfully pursue policies which reflect its rejection of Russia's war aims, maintain its foreign policy autonomy, and secure its sovereignty, all the while maintaining its close economic and security relationships with Russia. This has been quite impressive. However, both Russia and the West are hardening their respective positions. Multivectorism may still be possible under these circumstances, but it likely will become far more complicated in the future.

References

Abbasova, V. (2022, July 6). *Kazakhstan Voices Readiness to Help Ease Global Energy Crisis*. Caspian News. https://caspiannews.com/news-detail/kazakhstan-voices-readiness-to-help-ease-global-energy-crisis-2022-7-5-14/

Agence France-Presse. (2022, April 28). *Kazakhstan Set to Ban Russian Presenter Over Ukraine Tirade*. https://www.themoscowtimes.com/2022/04/28/kazakhstan-says-to-ban-russian-presenter-over-ukraine-tirade-a77527

Askar, A. (2022). *What's Next for Russians Who Fled to Kazakhstan?* The Diplomat. https://thediplomat.com/2022/11/whats-next-for-russians-who-fled-to-kazakhstan/

Altynbayev, K. (2022a, March 8). *Ukraine Invasion Prompts Kazakhs to Turn off Russian Media Outlets*. Caravanserai. https://central.asia-news.com/en_GB/articles/cnmi_ca/features/2022/03/08/feature-01

Altynbayev, K. (2022b, April 28). *Kazakhstan's Scrapping of Victory Day Parade Highlights Strained Russian Ties*. Caravanserai. https://central.asia-news.com/en_GB/articles/cnmi_ca/features/2022/04/28/feature-01

Ambrosio, T. (2021). Security Hedging After Nazarbayev? The Future of Kazakhstan's Alignment with Russia. In J.-F. Caron (Ed.), *Understanding Kazakhstan's 2019 Political Transition*. Palgrave.

Ambrosio, T. (2022). Belarus, Kazakhstan and Alliance Security Dilemmas in the Former Soviet Union: Intra-Alliance Threat and Entrapment After the Ukraine Crisis. *Europe Asia Studies*. https://doi.org/10.1080/09668136.2022.2061425

Ambrosio, T., & Lange, W. (2015). Mapping Kazakhstan's Geopolitical Code: Analysis of Nazarbayev's Presidential Addresses, 1997–2014. *Eurasian Geography and Economics, 55*(5), 537–559.

Beliakova, P. (2022, February 4). *How a Russian-Led Alliance Keeps a Lid on Central Asia*. War on the Rocks. https://warontherocks.com/2022/02/how-a-russian-led-alliance-keeps-a-lid-on-central-asia

Bezpalko, B. (2022, April 1). *Crazed Kazakhstan Turns into a Second Ukraine*. IA Regnum. https://regnum.ru/news/polit/3552717.html

Bhadrakumar, M. (2022, May 23). *CSTO Won't Be Drawn into Ukraine War*. News Click. https://www.newsclick.in/CSTO-wont-drawn-ukraine-war

Cadell, C., & Nakashima, E. (2022, June 2). Beijing Chafes at Moscow's Requests for Support, Chinese Officials Say. *Washington Post*. https://www.washingtonpost.com/national-security/2022/06/02/china-support-russia-ukraine/

"CSTO Summit." (2022, May 16). *President of Russia*. http://en.kremlin.ru/events/president/news/68418

de Haas, M. (2017). Relations of Central Asia with the Shanghai Cooperation Organization and the Collective Security Treaty Organization. *Journal of Slavic Military Studies, 30*(1), 1–16.

"Deputy Prosecutor General of the Republic of Kazakhstan B. B. Dembayev's Appeal in accordance with Article 31 of the Law 'On the Prosecutor's Office'" Kazakhstan Prosecutor General Office, March 28, https://www.gov.kz/memleket/entities/prokuror/press/news/details/346474?lang=kk

"Expansion of Partnership with Third Countries is Urgent—the President." (2022, May 27). *Kazinform*. https://www.inform.kz/kz/ushinshi-eldermen-seriktestikti-keneytu-ozekti-prezident_a3938002

Globe, P. (2022, April 5). *Moscow Outraged That Kazakhstan Becoming 'a Second Ukraine'*. Eurasia Daily Monitor. https://jamestown.org/program/moscow-outraged-that-kazakhstan-becoming-a-second-ukraine/

Gotev, G. (2022, March 29). *Kazakh Official: We Will Not Risk Being Placed in the Same Basket as Russia*. Euractiv. https://www.euractiv.com/section/central-asia/interview/kazakh-official-we-will-not-risk-being-placed-in-the-same-basket-as-russia/

Gleason, G. (2022, October 25). New Military Doctrine Strengthens Kazakhstan's Multi-vector Posture. *The Diplomat*. https://thediplomat.com/2022/10/new-military-doctrine-strengthens-kazakhstans-multi-vector-posture/

Hedenskog, J., & von Essen, H. (2022, January 14). *Russia's CSTO Intervention in Kazakhstan: Motives, Risks and Consequences*. SCEEUS. https://www.ui.se/forskning/centrum-for-osteuropastudier/sceeus-commentary/russias-csto-intervention-in-kazakhstan-motives-risks-and-consequences/

International Crisis Group. (2022, January 14). *Behind the Unrest in Kazakhstan*. https://www.crisisgroup.org/europe-central-asia/central-asia/kazakhstan/behind-unrest-kazakhstan

Judge, A., Maltby, T., & Sharples, J. D. (2016). Challenging Reductionism in Analyses of EU-Russia Energy Relations. *Geopolitics, 21*(1), 751–762.

"Kazakh Court Sentences Couple that Called for North Kazakhstan to Join Russia." (2022, August 3). *Radio Free Europe/Radio Liberty*. https://www.rferl.org/a/kazakh-court-sentences-couple-north-kazakhstan-russia/31972190.html

"Kazakhstan has no Plans to Revise Trade Relations with Russia within EAEU, says Minister." (2022, April 14). *TASS*. https://tass.com/economy/1437543

"Kazakhstan Inflation Rate." (2022). *Trading Economics*. https://tradingeconomics.com/kazakhstan/inflation-cpi

"Kazakhstan Marks Victory Day." (2022, May 10). *Xinhua*. http://en.people.cn/n3/2022/0510/c90000-10094347.html

"Kazakhstan MFA about the 'Referendum in Ukraine." (2022, September 26). *Radio Liberty* (*Azattyq radiosy*). https://www.azattyq.org/a/32052135.html

"Kazakhstan's President Addresses Challenging Issues on International Agenda and Relations with Russia at Saint Petersburg Economic Forum." (2022, June 18). *Kazakhstan Ministry of Foreign Affairs*. https://www.gov.kz/memleket/entities/mfa/press/news/details/390248?lang=en&fbclid=IwAR3hCPds9Al6gpNDKvajZWRTJOJMoNqXKQQpetersW5I2YeAORca-3ODqAkSJ_MoA

"Kazakhstan's Toqaev Tells Putin Russia Strategic Partner Despite Ukraine War." (2022a, November 28). *Radio Free Europe/Radio Liberty*. https://www.rferl.org/a/kazakhstan-russia-toqaev-putin-partners/32152374.html

"Kazakhstan's Toqaev Tells Putin Russia Strategic Partner Despite Ukraine War." (2022b). *RFE*.

Kumenov, A. (2022a, February 17). *Kazakhstan Plans to Increase Grain Exports Despite Harvest Woes*. Eurasianet. https://eurasianet.org/kazakhstan-plans-to-increase-grain-exports-despite-harvest-woes

Kumenov, A. (2022b, March 4). *Kazakhstan Redirecting Import-Export from Russia to Latvia*. Eurasianet. https://eurasianet.org/kazakhstan-redirecting-import-export-from-russia-to-latvia

Kumenov, A. (2022c, March 28). *Kazakhstan: Radio Presenter's Contentious Pro-Russia Barb Exposes Broader Anxieties*. Eurasianet. https://eurasianet.org/kazakhstan-radio-presenters-contentious-pro-russia-barb-exposes-broader-anxieties

Kumenov, A. (2022d, April 14). *Kazakhstan Bolsters Defenses Amid Russian Invasion of Ukraine*. Eurasianet. https://eurasianet.org/kazakhstan-bolsters-defenses-amid-russian-invasion-of-ukraine

Kumenov, A. (2022e, April 21). *Sanctioned Russian Banks Seeking Way Out of Kazakhstan*. Eurasianet. https://eurasianet.org/sanctioned-russian-banks-seeking-way-out-of-kazakhstan

Lautman, O. (2022, July 11). *Kazakhstan Thumbs Its Nose at Putin*. Center for European Policy Analysis. https://cepa.org/kazakhstan-thumbs-its-nose-at-putin/

Lillis, J., & Imanaliyeva, A. (2022, March 7). *Ukraine War Inspires Rival Passions in Central Asia*. Eurasianet. https://eurasianet.org/ukraine-war-inspires-rival-passions-in-central-asia

Marat, E., & Engvall, J. (2022, May 10). *Former Soviet States Are Distancing Themselves from Their Old Imperial Master*. Foreign Policy. https://foreignpolicy.com/2022/05/10/soviet-imperialism-colonialism-ukraine-kazakhstan-georgia-moldova/

Meduza. (2022, January 6). *From 'Demonstrators' to 'Terrorists' How Kazakhstani Officials Changed the Way they Talk About the Unrest now Sweeping the Nation*. https://meduza.io/en/feature/2022/01/06/from-demonstrators-to-terrorists

"Meeting with President of Kazakhstan Kassym-Jomart Tokayev." (2022, February 10). *President of Russia*. http://en.kremlin.ru/events/president/news/67748

Michel, C. (2022, January 6). *Kazakhstan's Border with Russia Is Suddenly an Open Question Again*. Foreign Policy. https://foreignpolicy.com/2022/01/06/kazakhstan-protests-russia-intervention-troops-ethnic-separatism-secession-ukraine/

Najibullah, F. (2014, September 3). *Putin Downplays Kazakh Independence, Sparks Angry Reaction*. Radio Free Europe/Radio Liberty. https://www.rferl.org/a/kazakhstan-putin-history-reactionnation/26565141.html

Nazarbayev, N. (1997, October 16). *Address of the President of the Republic of Kazakhstan*. President of Kazakhstan. http://www.akorda.kz/en/addresses/addresses_of_president/address-of-the-president-of-the-republic-of-kazakhstan-nursultan-nazarbayev-to-the-people-of-kazakhstan-october-10-1997

"Nursultan Nazarbayev Attended Victory Day Parade in Moscow." (2019, May 9). *Kazinform*. https://www.inform.kz/en/nursultan-nazarbayev-attended-victory-day-parade-in-moscow_a3524849

Nurgozhayeva, R. (2022, March 22). *Where Does Kazakhstan Stand on Russia's Invasion of Ukraine?* Jurist. https://www.jurist.org/commentary/2022/03/roza-nurgozhayeva-russia-ukraine-invasion-kazakhstan/

Nurmaganbetova, Z. (2022, May 5). *Kazakhstan to Increase Defense and Law Enforcement Agencies Funding*. Kazinform. https://www.inform.kz/en/kazakhstan-to-increase-defense-and-law-enforcement-agencies-funding_a3930122

"On amendments and additions to the Decree of the President of the Republic of Kazakhstan dated September 29, 2017 No. 554 'On approval of the Military Doctrine of the Republic of Kazakhstan'." (2022, October 12). *Kazakhstan Ministry of Justice*. https://adilet.zan.kz/kaz/docs/U2200001045

"On amendments to the Decree of the President of the Republic of Kazakhstan Dated September 29, 2017 No. 554 'On approval of the Military Doctrine of the Republic of Kazakhstan'." (2022, June 10). *Government of Kazakhstan*. https://legalacts.egov.kz/npa/view?id=14119675

"On the Talks Between Kazakh Foreign Minister and the US Secretary of State." (2022, May 21). *Government of Kazakhstan*. https://www.gov.kz/memleket/entities/mfa/press/news/details/375465?lang=en

Pannier, B. (2022, April 7). *Ukraine War Sparks Suspicion over Russia's Designs on Kazakhstan*. Foreign Policy Research Institute. https://www.fpri.org/article/2022/04/ukraine-war-sparks-suspicion-over-russias-designs-on-kazakhstan/

Prokhvatilov, V. (2022, June 4). *Which Side of the Iron Curtain Does Kazakhstan Want to Be on?* Strategic Culture Foundation. http://www.fondsk.ru/news/2022/04/06/po-kakyu-storonu-zheleznogo-zanavesa-hochet-byt-kazahstan-55925.html

Putz, C. (2022a, March 8). How Will the War in Ukraine Affect Central Asian Remittance Flows? *The Diplomat*. https://thediplomat.com/2022/03/how-will-the-war-in-ukraine-affect-central-asian-remittance-flows/

Putz, C. (2022b, April 28). 'Look at Ukraine': Russian Commentator Threatens Kazakhstan. *The Diplomat*. https://thediplomat.com/2022/04/look-at-ukraine-russian-commentator-threatens-kazakhstan/

Putz, C. (2022c, June 15). Tokayev Downplays January CSTO Deployment to Kazakhstan. *The Diplomat*. https://thediplomat.com/2022/06/tokayev-downplays-january-csto-deployment-to-kazakhstan/

Putz, C. (2022d, November 28). Kazakhstan Walks Diplomatic Tightrope Between Russia and Europe. *The Diplomat*. https://thediplomat.com/2022/11/kazakhstan-walks-diplomatic-tightrope-between-russia-and-europe/

Rickleton, C. (2022, April 4). *Kazakhstan Seeks to Thread Diplomatic Needle over Russia's Ukraine War*. Eurasianet. https://eurasianet.org/kazakhstan-seeks-to-thread-diplomatic-needle-over-russias-ukraine-war

Ruehl, J. (2022, January 29). *Why It's Time to Take the Russian-Led Military Alliance Seriously*. Independent Media Institute. https://www.pressenza.com/2022/01/why-its-time-to-take-the-russian-led-military-alliance-seriously/

"Russia Reverses Course on Oil Pipeline Needed by Kazakhastan." (2022, July 11). *Eurasianet*. https://eurasianet.org/russia-reverses-course-on-oil-pipeline-needed-by-kazakhstan

"Russian Journalists Accuse Kazakhstan of Ingratitude for Attempting to Maintain Relations with both Russia and the West." (2022, April 27). *MEMRI*. https://www.memri.org/reports/russian-journalists-accuse-kazakhstan-ingratitude-attempting-maintain-relations-both-russia

Sánchez, A., & Auyezova, K. (2022, May 11). *Kazakhstan Cancels Victory Day in Protest over Putin's Ukraine War*. Atlantic Council. https://www.atlanticcouncil.org/blogs/ukrainealert/kazakhstan-cancels-victory-day-in-protest-over-putins-ukraine-war/

Satubaldina, A. (2022, April 25). *Kazakh Delegation Visits US to Reaffirm Strategic Partnership, Discuss Impact of Sanctions*. Astana Times. https://astanatimes.com/2022/04/kazakh-delegation-visits-us-to-reaffirm-strategic-partnership-discuss-impact-of-sanctions/

Šćepanović, J. (2022, June 13). *The Sheriff and the Banker? Russia and China in Central Asia*. War on the Rocks. https://warontherocks.com/2022/06/the-sheriff-and-the-banker-russia-and-china-in-central-asia/

"Session of CSTO Collective Security Council." (2022, January 10). *President of Russia*. http://en.kremlin.ru/events/president/news/67568

"St Petersburg International Economic Forum Plenary Session 2022." President of Russia, June 17. http://en.kremlin.ru/events/president/news/68669

Shapoo, S. (2022, April 18). *Could Kazakhstan Suffer the Same Fate as Ukraine?*. National Interest. https://nationalinterest.org/blog/buzz/could-kazakhstan-suffer-same-fate-ukraine-201882

Siheon Nathaniel Choi, S., Buranelli, F., & Fumagalli, M. (2022, February 13). *What the CSTO's Intervention in Kazakhstan Really Means*. https://nationalinterest.org/print/feature/what-csto%E2%80%99s-intervention-kazakhstan-really-means-200487

Simes, D. (2022, January 15). *Russian-led CSTO's Kazakhstan Mission Leaves Lingering Bootprints*. Nikkei Asia. https://asia.nikkei.com/Politics/International-relations/Russian-led-CSTO-s-Kazakhstan-mission-leaves-lingering-bootprints

Sorbello, P. (2022, August 5). Former Russian President Questions Kazakhstan's Sovereignty. *The Diplomat*. https://thediplomat.com/2022/08/former-russian-president-questions-kazakhstans-sovereignty/

"Statement by the Collective Security Treaty Organization Collective Security Treaty Organization on the Occasion of the 30th Anniversary of the Collective Security Treaty and the 20th Anniversary of the Collective Security Treaty Organization." (2022, May 16). *CSTO*. https://odkb-csto.org/documents/statements/zayavlenie-soveta-kollektivnoy-bezopasnosti-organizatsii-dogovora-o-kollektivnoy-bezopasnosti-v-svya/#loaded

Stronski, P. (2022, March 30). *The Common Theme in Central Asia's Response to Russia's Invasion of Ukraine*. Carnegie Endowment for International Peace. https://carnegieendowment.org/2022/03/30/common-theme-in-central-asia-s-response-to-russia-s-invasion-of-ukraine-pub-86764

Sullivan, C. (2019). End of an Era? Kazakhstan and the Fate of Multivectorism. In J.-F. Caron (Ed.), *Kazakhstan and the Soviet Legacy* (pp. 31–5). Palgrave Macmillan

Tazhutov, A. (2022, April 1). *Kazakhstan Faces 'Threat of Losing Its Statehood'?* Eurasia Review. https://www.eurasiareview.com/01042022-kazakhstan-faces-threat-of-losing-its-statehood-oped/

"The Republic of Kazakhstan launched the active phase of the command and staff training of the Collective Security Treaty Organization 'Interaction-2022', special trainings 'Search-2022' and 'Echelon-2022'." (2022, October 3). *Collective Security Treaty Organization*. https://en.odkb-csto.org/news/news_odkb/v-kazakhstane-dan-start-aktivnoy-faze-komandno-shtabnogo-ucheniya-ksor-odkb-vzaimodeystvie-2022-spets/#loaded

"The Movement of Military Equipment around the Country Takes Place as Part of the Exercise." (2022, April 7). *Kazakhstan Ministry of Defense*. https://www.gov.kz/memleket/entities/mod/press/news/details/352301?lang=en

Tokayev, K.-J. (2022, April 4). *Turbulence Across Eurasia Will Not Slow Kazakhstan's Progress*. National Interest. https://nationalinterest.org/feature/turbulence-across-eurasia-will-not-slow-kazakhstan%E2%80%99s-progress-201591

Umarov, T. (2022, August 10). *After Ukraine, Is Kazakhstan Next in the Kremlin's Sights?* Carnegie Endowment for International Peace. https://carnegieendowment.org/eurasiainsight/87652

Volkmann-Schluck, P. (2022, April 4). *How Putin 'Lost' Kazakhstan, and Squashed His Own Soviet Revival*. Die Welt. https://www.welt.de/politik/ausland/plus237816257/Kasachstan-und-Russland-Wie-Putin-seinen-Sowjet-Traum-zerstoert.html

Waal, T. (2022). "Kazakhstan does not Support Russia or Ukraine -- Ministry of Defense," Vlast, March 3, https://vlast.kz/novosti/48974-kazahstan-ne-pod derzivaet-ni-rossiu-ni-ukrainu-minoborony.html

From Qandy Qantar to Tragic January: State Framing of the January Events

Akbota Karibayeva and Edward Lemon

Abstract For 30 years, Kazakhstan's government prided itself on being the most stable and economically successful country in Central Asia. The January 2022 unrest shook up that image of stability and prosperity. Faced with a serious threat to his regime's survival, President Tokayev took a number of exceptional measures in an effort to quell the violence and restore order. First, on January 5, he cut off all access to the internet and mobile phone networks after announcing a nationwide state of emergency. Second, at the invitation of the government of Kazakhstan, peacekeeping forces of the Collective Security Treaty Organization (CSTO), a Russian-led regional security alliance, were deployed to stabilize the situation. Third, Tokayev declared that the violent rioters were connected to foreign terrorist and criminal organizations and gave a "shoot-to-kill without warning" order against the protesters on January 7. These actions

A. Karibayeva (✉)
George Washington University, Washington, DC, USA
e-mail: akaribayeva@gwu.edu

E. Lemon
Texas A&M University, College Station, TX, USA
e-mail: edward.lemon@tamu.edu

J.-F. Caron (ed.), *A Revolt in the Steppe*, The Steppe and Beyond: Studies on Central Asia,
https://doi.org/10.1007/978-981-99-0783-0_4

came at a high cost to Kazakhstan's reputation, undermining the regime's legitimacy in the eyes of domestic and international audiences. How does a state deal with reputational and legitimacy costs of protest repression when the dust settles? In this chapter, we explore the dynamic of the Tokayev administration's attempt at damage control through strategic narrative framing. We conduct a critical discourse analysis of Tokayev's speeches and tweets and demonstrate how the government scripted a hegemonic narrative designed to justify the measures it took during the crisis, adjusted the narrative in response to public pushback, and framed the unrest as a teaching moment that ushered in a "New Kazakhstan."

Keywords Protest · Strategic narrative · Framing · Legitimacy · Kazakhstan

For 30 years, Kazakhstan's government prided itself on being the most stable and economically successful country in Central Asia, "an oasis of stability in an otherwise uncertain world" (Lewis, 2016, p. 424). Under the leadership of Nursultan Nazarbayev (1989–2019) and his successor Kassym-Zhomart Tokayev (2019–present), the government legitimized its authoritarian rule by stressing its central and essential role in building stability and prosperity in the country. Kazakhstan adopted a policy of authoritarian modernization, insisting that economic reforms that bolster living standards should come before any political liberalization (Foa, 2018). The government capitalized on its resource wealth to generate support by prioritizing economics over other aspects of public policy, posting growth rates averaging 10% in the first decade of the 2000s. Relying on this wealth, the government built a new modernist capital city, Astana, organized mega-events such as the 2017 Expo, and launched various initiatives to promote itself as a hub for dialogue, including hosting peace talks on Syria and Ukraine and a triannual summit for religious leaders—the Congress of Leaders of World and Traditional Religions (Fauve, 2015; Omelicheva, 2016; Valiyev & Valiyev, 2015). This carefully-cultivated image of stability and prosperity has been challenged on a number of occasions, most notably during the outbreak of violence in December 2011 in the provincial city of Zhanaozen, in which 14 striking oil workers were killed by law enforcement (Lewis, 2016).

But the events of January 2022 posed the greatest challenge to the regime in the country's independent history. Faced with a serious threat to his regime survival, Tokayev took various exceptional measures in an effort to quell the violence. First, on January 5, he announced a nationwide state of emergency, cutting off access to the internet and mobile phone networks. Second, at the invitation of the government of Kazakhstan, peacekeeping forces of the Collective Security Treaty Organization (CSTO), a Russian-led regional security alliance, was deployed to stabilize the situation (Kucera, 2022). Third, Tokayev declared that the violent rioters were connected to foreign terrorist and criminal organizations and gave a "shoot-to-kill without warning" order against the protesters on January 7 (Ilyushina & Cheng, 2022).

A prolonged communication shutdown, the use of violence against peaceful protesters, and the intervention of foreign troops to resolve the situation all had unprecedentedly high material and reputational repercussions for a regime that had built its legitimacy on being "softer" than many of its neighbors (Schatz, 2009; Schatz & Maltseva, 2012). These high-cost measures significantly undermined the government's legitimacy in the eyes of domestic and international audiences. As President Tokayev admitted in March 2022, "the events of "Tragic January" have already caused serious damage to the reputation of our country." Tokayev conducted damage control by employing various framing techniques to rationalize the costly responses to the public. The state crafted a narrative that justified and humanized its responses by presenting the state as only tactically reacting to the situation on the ground while acting in the interests of the people at large. The government attempted to script a hegemonic narrative that justified the measures it took during the crisis, adjusted the narrative in response to pushback, and framed the unrest as a teaching moment that ushered in a "New Kazakhstan."

This chapter explores how the government framed the January events, how these frames helped justify the exceptional measures taken, how the narrative shifted over time, and how the government tried to spin events in a positive way to reinforce the regime and reduce the post-factum audience costs of repression. We focus on two aspects of the framing. First, the rhetorical repertoire deployed by the government demonstrates a carefully chosen set of frames aimed to resonate with the public audience. For example, by labeling rioters as terrorists, the government appealed to the public concern for safety, which gave it carte blanche for radical actions, such as the shoot-to-kill order. Second, rather than being fixed, it evolved in response to public pushback. The government adjusted its narrative to accommodate discursive pushback while staying within the main legitimizing frames. For example, after civil society voiced criticism for cracking down on peaceful protesters, the government adopted a disclaimer, stating that there were indeed peaceful protesters whom the law enforcement treated with restraint, and that it was only after the protests were hijacked by well-trained terrorists and bandits that the government authorized the use of force.

Authoritarian Legitimacy in a Time of Crisis

Authoritarian governance rests on three pillars: repression, co-optation, and legitimacy (Gerschewski, 2013). Of the three, legitimation has been the least studied (Gerschewski & Dukalskis, 2017; Mayer, 2001; von Soest & Grauvogel, 2015; Zhao, 2009). Legitimation seeks to guarantee the population's "active consent, compliance with the rules, passive obedience, or mere toleration" of the regime (Gerschewski, 2013, p. 18; Gerschewski & Dukalskis, 2017). Modes of legitimation include government performance, the deployment of ideology, state-controlled narratives on collective history, and external legitimation (Omelicheva, 2016).

Authoritarian legitimation relies on the construction of a hegemonic discourse that is internalized by key social groups. The government and its allies develop and deploy specific ideas, narratives, and frames that control how issues and their solutions are presented, as well as restrict the "possibility of articulating alternatives to the political status quo" (Lewis, 2016, p. 422). Ideally, these narratives resonate with social attitudes and opinions, creating what David Rampton has called "deeper hegemony" (Rampton, 2011). As a result, the audience internalizes and accepts them as "common sense" (Gramsci, 1971, pp. 321–331). As van Dijk argues, "dominance may be enacted and reproduced by subtle, routine, everyday forms of text and talk that appear 'natural' and quite 'acceptable'" (van Dijk, 1993, p. 254). Ultimately, legitimation enables authoritarian regimes to rule through consent rather than pure coercion.

In light of the increasing reputational costs of coercive control, authoritarian regimes have developed what Guriev and Triesman call "informational autocracy," where autocrats rely on surgical manipulation of information to convince the domestic population of their competence and maintain legitimacy (Guriev & Treisman, 2019). They posit that authoritarians employ the rhetoric of economic development and public service provision to win citizens' approval. "Informational autocrats" take advantage of available tools of traditional and online media control to skew public discourse and shape perceptions to their favor, thereby promoting regime durability (Gunitsky, 2015). Such messaging is both internally and externally oriented. Even the most illiberal authoritarians, including governments of China, Russia, and Saudi Arabia, hire consulting companies, such as McKinsey & Company, to "improve their international reputations and whitewash their human rights records" (Morgenbesser, 2020, p. 1058), a process Dukalskis calls "authoritarian image management" (Dukalskis, 2021). They sponsor established Western think tanks to project a favorable image abroad, co-opt and incentivize public figures to encourage popular support, and conscript armies of trolls to undercut domestic critics (Morgenbesser, 2020).

Moments of regime destabilization, such as the 1989 Tiananmen Square protests in China or the Arab Spring, cause this hegemonic narrative to be disrupted. Torfing calls this "discursive dislocation," defined as "a destabilization of a discourse that results from the emergence of events which cannot be domesticated, symbolized or integrated within the discourse in question" (Torfing, 1999, p. 301). Academics have termed such uses of unprecedented levels of violence by the state "severe repression" (Sutton et al., 2014), "severe state-sponsored violence" (Carey, 2010), and "inconsistent repression" (Francisco, 2005). Using examples from violence in Tajikistan (2008–2011) and Kazakhstan (2011), Erica Marat calls this interruption of typical repression patterns "transformative violence," an unprecedented use of violence that ushers in broader political changes and offers opportunities for regimes to expand their coercive control (Marat, 2016; Tilly, 2003). Yet, the way authoritarian regimes justify repression during times of crisis has received little scholarly attention (Dukalskis, 2017; Edel & Josua, 2018).

In the context of Central Asia, Nick Megoran's work on the framing of the 2005 Andijan massacre argues that Karimov's government framed the protestors at Andijan as criminals intent on undermining the constitutional order and subverting the government's gradualist approach to reform (Megoran, 2008). In a book dedicated to the massacre, President Islam Karimov framed it as a "law and order operation in reaction to a plot perpetrated by criminals and terrorists of deviant masculinity, religiosity and inauthentic nationality, opposed to the constitutional order and at odds with the scientific laws of states" (Megoran, 2008, p. 28).

The social movements literature on framing mainly focuses on social movements' strategic use of frames to inspire mobilization, primarily treating the state as a passive respondent to those frames (Ferree, 2003; Johnston, 2005). Looking at state reactions during protests, Bishara (2015) explores the dynamics of ignoring, where the government intentionally acts dismissively toward popular mobilization to delegitimize it and facilitate demobilization. Chang and Vitale (2013) examine how the likelihood of repression varies in response to situational and strategic variables, suggesting that "weak status" movements that challenge the regime's legitimacy are more likely to be repressed. Koopmans (2005) views repression as a form of "strategic communication in the public sphere" and argues that discursive opportunities play an important role in determining the levels and nature of state repression in response to protest mobilization. In short, the state reacts to challengers differently depending on their visibility, resonance, and legitimacy in the eyes of the public. State responses to protest events should therefore be viewed as strategic and performative in nature.

This literature on authoritarian image management in times of crisis forms part of a broader literature on authoritarian conflict management and illiberal forms of peacebuilding (de Oliveira, 2011; Heathershaw & Mullojonov, 2018; Lewis et al., 2018; Owen et al., 2018). These authoritarian approaches place emphasis on order and hierarchy rather than freedom and equality (Smith et al., 2020). Authoritarian conflict management aims to maintain regime survival by preventing rebels from influencing public discourse, controlling resources, and shaping political space (Heathershaw & Owen, 2019). A sovereign dictator needs to act decisively, and extra-legally if necessary, to bring about order by addressing external threats. In the area of discourse, authoritarian regimes develop a hegemonic narrative about the causes and appropriate responses to the unrest, at the same time preventing opponents from influencing the discourse. The goal is to create "shared discourses" that bond the regime to the majority of the population at the exclusion of those articulating alternatives (Owen et al., 2018, p. 13).

Kazakhstan's "Listening State"

Under Nazarbayev, Kazakhstan developed a regime based on a framework by which the state provides technocratic solutions to their problem, what Assel Rustemova and Laura Adams called "managerial governmentality" (Adams & Rustemova, 2009). The state managed society through limited regulation and encouraging citizens to pursue self-enrichment (Insebayeva & Insebayeva, 2021). However, while they were given autonomy to pursue their individual economic goals, the model was top-down, leaving little room for the citizens to have any say in governance.

When he came to power in March 2019, Tokayev did not break from this performance-based legitimation model, but he introduced his own interpretation of it known as the Listening State. According to Tokayev, "our common task is to implement the concept of the "Listening State," which quickly and efficiently responds to all constructive citizen requests. Only through a constant dialogue between the Government and society can a harmonious state be built in the context of modern geopolitics" (Akorda, 2019). The Listening State claims to produce a more accountable government by allowing citizens to voice complaints and even have officials removed. But adjudicating which citizen demands are "constructive" and legitimate still remains the state's prerogative. The Listening State remains a vague concept, supposedly aimed at constraining state officials and increasing accountability. In July 2019, the government established a National Council of Public Trust to channel public requests to officials. However, the body maintains a consultative status and consists of the members of society approved by the office of the president, continuing the approach of "state-managed public discourse" (Karibayeva & Meyer, 2022). Ultimately, there is little evidence that the Listening State is about genuinely increasing government accountability. Instead, it is a legitimation strategy that allows the government to maintain a facade of responsiveness when in reality the system remains deeply authoritarian.

This hegemonic narrative of state-society dialogue and harmony was starting to unravel in the run up to January 2022. According to the Central Asia Protest Tracker, protests in Kazakhstan surged from 47 in 2018 to 524 in the first half of 2021 alone (Aisarina et al., 2021). Protests spiked at times such as elections, with demonstrations taking place in multiple cities coordinated by opposition groups such as the Democratic Party and the Democratic Choice of Kazakhstan, and social movements such as Oyan Qazaqstan. These rising tensions between society and the state broke out into the largest protests in the country's history in January 2022.

Methodology

In our analysis, we focus on 12 speeches that President Tokayev gave between January 5 and March 16 as well as tweets posted on his official Twitter page @TokaevKZ.[1] Six were in a mix of Kazakh and Russian, two were fully in Kazakh, three were fully in Russian, and one was in English. We used critical discourse analysis to analyze the speeches, adopting Norman Fairclough's three-step approach which involves analyzing the text itself, how it fits with the larger discourse of texts, and whether the text reproduces or challenges the dominant relations of power (Fairclough, 1992, p. 73). We chose to analyze the speeches of President Tokayev because he was vocal throughout the crisis, making frequent speeches. Tokayev was also the prime producer of the hegemonic narrative; his speeches set the tone for other government statements.

Framing Bloody January

As unrest spread around the country in January 2022, the President took a number of exceptional measures that had reputational costs. In justifying these measures, the government used a number of narrative frames which combined to form the core narrative. The framing strategies appealed to culturally contextualized frames that created collective identities, delegitimized alternative narratives, and strategically emphasized different messages to different audiences. The state worked to promote the core narrative by mobilizing its communication resources to increase visibility and discursive dominance over alternative accounts. The state employed framing strategies to put forward an alternative account of what happened, what these events mean (or should mean) for different actors and the target audience, who is to blame and who deserves empathy. We deconstruct the narrative-building process following Benford and Snow's framework of diagnostic, prognostic, and motivational framing (Benford & Snow, 2000).

Diagnostic framing involves problem identification and attribution (Benford & Snow, 2000, p. 615). Frame articulators propose their version of what happened and what role and responsibility each actor had. Tokayev started his speeches with a summary of the current situation on the ground. He narrated the events around a number of frames. First, he

[1] For a full list, see Appendix.

labeled the events as being perpetrated by "terrorists" who were seeking to destabilize the country. Tokayev repeatedly labeled the participants in the protests "bandits" (*bandity*), "marauders" (*marodery*), "terrorists" (terroristy), "pirates" (*piraty*), and "foreign fighters" (*zarubezhniye boeviki*) who were bent on "seizing power." As Tokayev stated, "bandits, terrorists arrived in Almaty from outside. The goal is known: murder, intimidation, robbery of shops, rape of women and, in the end, the overthrow of power" (Transcript 10). Second, he stressed that the groups driving the unrest were organized, part of a well-planned conspiracy to overthrow the government. In explaining the events, Tokayev placed the blame on his predecessor Nursultan Nazarbayev:

> Thanks to the First President, Elbasy, a group of very profitable companies and a layer of people who are rich even by international standards have emerged in the country. I believe that the time has come to make it right by the people of Kazakhstan and support them on a systematic and regular basis. (Transcript 5)

Third, he linked these groups to foreign sponsors. Amid these vivid descriptions of large-scale destruction that covered half of the country, Tokayev portrays the law enforcement personnel as having little agency, the state as having no responsibility in the escalation, and himself as a seeker of order who repeatedly but unsuccessfully tried to calm down the perpetrators.

Prognostic framing aims to articulate a strategy to solve the problem, "what is to be done" (Benford & Snow, 2000, p. 616). By highlighting the disconnect between what is going on and how it should be, the state identifies and rationalizes the solution it devises. As Tokayev stated, "my constitutional duty is that I must take care of the wellbeing and security and peace of mind of our citizens" (Transcript 1). His actions were, in his framing, mere reactions to citizens' request to "urgently help them" by restoring peace and security. It is his responsibility to do what is in the best interest of the people, even if it means resorting to harsh measures and requesting CSTO assistance. At the same time, having labelled the protesters as terrorists, Tokayev discredited the alternative solution of peacefully resolving the conflict as complete "nonsense" (Transcript 3). Indeed, it is a widely shared normative position that negotiating with terrorists is not a viable policy option.

Motivational framing prompts action by providing a rationale for audience engagement and prescribes what this engagement should look like. Since the state's objective primarily involved demobilization and de-escalation, Tokayev's messaging to the domestic audience focused on discouraging citizens from joining the riot crowds and eliciting support for the chosen repressive measures:

> Once again, I appeal to you to show prudence and not succumb to internal and external provocations, the euphoria of rallies, and permissiveness. Calls to attack the premises of civilian and military agencies are absolutely illegal. This is a crime, and legal punishment will follow. [...] I appeal to young people: do not ruin your lives and the lives of your loved ones. (Transcript 2)

Tokayev called for unity, suggesting that the key to overcoming this challenge and recovering from the tragedy that happened to Kazakhstan is to stand together in solidarity with the state. While encouraging patience and non-involvement, Tokayev also discouraged those likely to join the unrest through prescriptive, somewhat threatening messages: "show prudence," "do not succumb" to provocations, "do not ruin your lives" by mobilizing.

Tokayev also used connectors like "therefore" and "in light of this" to walk the audience through his train of thought, the logic behind the actions, thereby using state response as a means of bridging the current problem (chaos and lack of security) with the desired outcome (order and security). This sequence of frames had an important narrative-building implication. Starting by framing the problem as a security threat to civilians and the state, Tokayev instilled concern and fear before offering a solution to the problem. When framed this way, such radical measures as authorizing a "shoot to kill without warning" do not sound as radical anymore. We next unpack how these frames were deployed to justify Tokayev's exceptional measures.

Exceptional Measure 1: Communications Shutdown

On January 2, the government started shutting down the internet and mobile phone networks in the country. For more than a week, except

for short breaks of a few hours, people could not access websites, applications, or messenger apps. State-owned Kazakhtelecom controls the country's main internet service provider (ISP), and the security services own the only internet exchange point (IXP), allowing the government to enforce the blackout. The 2012 Law on National Security of the Republic of Kazakhstan stipulates that "when conducting anti-terrorist operations and curbing riots, by decision of the head of operational headquarters, network owners and communication operators may be given mandatory instructions to suspend the provision of communication services to individuals and (or) legal entities and (or) restrict network use and communications mode of operation of networks and means of communication" (Government of Kazakhstan, 2012).

Internet and mobile communication shutdowns have been an increasingly popular tool of authoritarian protest management (Feldstein, 2022). Although authoritarian states are known to preemptively deploy partial or full blocking of social media platforms and messengers to preclude popular mobilization in anticipation of possible protests—for example, during post-election periods—full communications shutdown during active protests is seen as a radical "last-straw response to mobilized masses" (Keremoğlu & Weidmann, 2020, p. 1695).

Such a strategy of protest management is appealing to governments for several reasons. First, protesters can use social media to provide information that can encourage others to join. By sharing updates on considerable turnout and peaceful conduct of protests, participants can signal their chances of success (Larson, 2019). Indeed, social media and mobile networks allowed for the quick diffusion of January protests from Zhanaozen to many other cities across the country. Blocking internet and mobile communication reduces the exchange of critical information about the progression of protests, making further mobilization unlikely (Gohdes, 2020). Second, social media and news updates on the internet and through messengers facilitate protest coordination (Tufekci & Wilson, 2012). For example, members of Oyan Qazaqstan, an activist group that mobilized some of the initial protests in Almaty, posted updates on the progression of their march. Blocking all communication leaves protesters with a very limited ability to coordinate. Finally, the internet allows protesters to spread the word to both domestic and international audiences (Larson, 2019). Shutting down communications gave the government an opportunity to control the narrative around the protests.

Despite these incentives, the full communications blackout came with considerable economic and reputational costs. Most businesses chose to suspend operations for the period of unrest, while many ordinary citizens were left without means of buying groceries as no bank terminals were functional to process online or in-store card payments (Orisbayev, 2022). According to some estimates, the January blackout amounted to 142 hours, affected more than 16 million users, and cost the Kazakhstani economy $429.5 million in lost business activity (Woodhams & Migliano, 2022). There were also reputational costs, with human rights watchdogs and democratic governments criticizing the Kazakhstani government for denying citizens their right to internet and telecommunication access (Freedom House, 2022).

In his speeches, President Tokayev framed the internet shutdown as a necessary measure to prevent the flow of disinformation. Tokayev concluded that "despite all the facts presented, some sources allege about the struggle of the authorities in Kazakhstan with peaceful demonstrators. This is absolute disinformation" (Transcript 4). He claimed that in "no case should we allow an information vacuum to be filled by provocateurs or ill-wishers" (Transcript 4). The government made it clear who was responsible. Tokayev took aim at the "so-called 'free' media and 'foreign' figures, who are far from the fundamental interests of our multinational people, were an accomplice in and, in fact, played an instigating role in violations of law and order" (Transcript 3). He argued that internet access entails responsibilities. According to Tokayev, "free access to the internet does not mean the free placement of fabrications, slander, insults, inflammatory appeals" (Transcript 3). In framing events in such a way, Tokayev shifted blame for the information shutdown to others, portraying it as a necessary measure to restore control, law, and order.

Exceptional Measure 2: Shoot-to-Kill Order

On January 7, President Tokayev appeared on television to announce that he had authorized the use of lethal force against those involved in the unrest. The move was risky. First, despite an expectation that violent repression should decrease protest participation, empirical evidence shows that it can also inspire greater mobilization. Ironically, the state use of force against dissidents can sometimes be perceived as a sign of weakness and, hence, an opening opportunity for protest escalation (Davenport, 2005, p. xx). Second, resorting to violence with the highest death toll in the 30-year history of independent Kazakhstan bears high legitimacy repercussions. Deadly clashes of the January events made the headlines of multiple global outlets highlighting a brutal authoritarian crackdown. The international community, including the United Nations Commission on Human Rights, Organization for Security and Cooperation in Europe, and the European Union, responded with statements condemning acts of violence and calling for respect of human rights.

The government deployed a number of frames to justify the order. According to Tokayev, "under the guise of spontaneous protests, a wave of riots unfolded. Religious radicals, criminal elements, notorious bandits, marauders, and petty hooligans operated as if under a single command" (Transcript 4). This notion that the events were "conspired" (*zamysel*) and "prepared" (*podgotovka*) can be seen throughout the hegemonic narrative (Transcripts 1, 5). The goal of the participants, according to the government, was to "undermine the constitutional order, to destroy the institutions of government, to seize power" (Transcript 4). He likened the situation to Syria, where "terrorists tried to capture Damascus and Raqqa" (Transcript 9). Such a framing of the participants as terrorists meant there was no room for negotiation:

> Voices from abroad call for negotiation of a peaceful solution. What nonsense! What kind of negotiations can there be with criminals and murderers?.. These are bandits and terrorists. They must be eliminated [...] I have given the order to law enforcement agencies and the army to open fire to kill without warning. (Transcript 3)

The displays of force cultivated the image of a strong and capable state, sending a credible signal of resolve and commitment to restoring order at all costs. In this environment, President Tokayev's "shoot-to-kill without warning" order served as a formal "legal" cover and final warning to protesters.

Exceptional Measure 3: Collective Security Treaty Organization Intervention

The Collective Security Treaty Organization (CSTO) is a regional military alliance. Its members include Armenia, Belarus, Kazakhstan, Kyrgyzstan, Russia, and Tajikistan. Article 4 of the Collective Security Treaty establishes that an act of aggression against one signatory is considered aggression against all. Until January 2022, numerous members had called for interventions under Article 4; the Kyrgyz government requested assistance from the CSTO in 2010 during ethnic conflict, and Armenia called for intervention numerous times in its ongoing conflict with Azerbaijan. But each time, the CSTO refused to intervene as these situations did not fall under its mandate.

On January 5, Tokayev made a televised address in which he claimed the participants had been "trained abroad, and their attack on Kazakhstan can and should be considered as an act of aggression" (Transcript 1). Tokayev claimed that "a terrorist war was unleashed against our country" (Transcript 5). In doing so, he justified an Article 4 intervention by the CSTO. On January 6, Secretary General of the CSTO Stanislav Zas stated that 2,500 troops from the Collective Peacekeeping Force were being deployed to Kazakhstan. The aim of the intervention, the CSTO stated, was the "protection of important state and military facilities, assistance to the law enforcement forces of the Republic of Kazakhstan in stabilizing the situation and returning it to the legal field" (CSTO, 2022). They were deployed to critical sites such as the Almaty airport, city hall, and others. With the situation under control, the forces began withdrawing on January 13.

The CSTO intervention in response to Tokayev's request served two purposes. First, it supplied military reinforcement and ensured the restoration of control over the strategic infrastructure. Second, and possibly most importantly, it demonstrated a symbolic external endorsement of neighboring governments. By signaling willingness and resolve to militarily support Tokayev, the CSTO intervention dispelled any doubts about the survival of his regime. This made any resistance of regime challengers, therefore, seem futile, contributing to final de-escalation and demobilization.

The intervention of foreign troops on Kazakhstani territory was damaging to the government on at least two levels. First, it was an admission of regime weakness, indicating that Tokayev had lost control over the situation and could not trust law enforcement. By calling on the CSTO to intervene, Tokayev placed himself with the likes of Kurmanbek Bakiyev in Kyrgyzstan in 2010 and Alexander Lukashenka in 2019, both of whom sought support for their regimes from Russia at a time of mass protest. He admitted the state had lost its monopoly on violence. Second, by inviting in Russian troops in particular, the government turned a national crisis into a matter of regional security and raised fears that this would be part of a longer-term occupation of Kazakh territory. The involvement of Russian troops in their former Soviet colony, an area that the Russian government still considers its principled sphere of influence, drew criticism from some. Third, the intervention raised questions as to what the Russian government would want in return for supporting the Tokayev regime (Askar, 2022). Speaking to the BBC, Russian analyst Arkady Dubnov predicted that going forward "the decisions of the leadership of Kazakhstan related to the orientation towards external centers of power—the US, the European Union, China, Turkey—will be made taking into account how Moscow may react to this" (BBC News, 2022). Some speculated that Kazakhstan would be expected to recognize Crimea as part of Russia (MK, 2022) and that this "ends the era of multivectorism in Kazakhstani foreign policy" (Anceschi, 2022). Overall, the move signaled the government's inability to control its domestic sphere and raised questions about Kazakhstan's sovereignty, generating significant reputational costs as a result.

In his speeches, Tokayev attempted to manage these concerns. Tokayev claimed that the exceptional nature of the circumstances on January 5 and the potential for much worse violence justified his decision to invite the CSTO to intervene:

> Since it was an armed aggression by international terrorism against our country, Kazakhstan is legally justified to appeal to its partners in the Collective Security Treaty with a request to send a peacekeeping contingent. It must be understood that at the time of making such a decision, we could completely lose control over Almaty, which would simply be given to the terrorists. If we lost Almaty, we would lose the capital and then the whole country. (Transcript 5)

He thanked the "moral support of partners in the CSTO" and expressed "special words of gratitude to the President of the Russian Federation Vladimir Vladimirovich Putin" (Transcript 4).

Evolving Discourse

Despite the strategic planning put into carefully crafting the initial narrative to make it resonate and to best sell the version of events that benefits the state most, the process of narrative framing was relational and evolutionary. The state as a frame articulator cannot just impose any narrative onto the audience (Benford & Snow, 2000, p. 625). Instead, the narrative must be validated and accepted by the audience for it to achieve hegemony. An analysis of Tokayev's speeches over time reveals an evolution of the narrative in response to popular pushback toward a more nuanced and balanced version. Although there remain major points of contestation between civil society and the state, as soon as the quorum of audiences has accepted the core assumptions of the narrative, the narrative locks in its relative equilibrium.

The first notable adjustment of the narrative concerns the acknowledgment of peaceful protesters. The early speeches of January 5 and 7 (Transcripts 1, 2, and 3) essentially reduce all non-state actors to armed rioters—terrorists and bandits. Tokayev even referred to them as "individuals who call themselves "protesters" (Transcript 1), thereby taking away the legitimacy of the actual peaceful protesters who originally started the wave of demonstrations around the country on January 2. Yet, after a wave of pushback from domestic and foreign media,[2] starting in his January 11 parliamentary address, Tokayev began differentiating between three stages of the January events, each dominated by a separate group of actors. "At the first round, rallies took place in a number of regions, in particular, in Zhanaozen. On the second, bandits and marauders joined. This was followed by a 'hot' phase, already with the participation of armed terrorists, including foreign fighters" (Transcript 5). This differentiation between actors was also accompanied by a rejection of a common allegation about the state use of force against peaceful protesters (Transcript 8). Instead, it was terrorists and bandits who impersonated the police:

> There was no and could not be any use of force against the peaceful demonstrators... The police did not carry weapons. They were only armed with stun grenades, tear gas, and water cannons. As for the cannons, they were seen used because they were immediately captured by bandits, [who] knew that the police had clear instructions not to use force against the so-called demonstrators. (Transcript 8)

Second, the CSTO intervention received domestic and foreign criticism, raising the question of owing a favor to Putin for stepping in and quickly mobilizing collective security forces. Naturally, this was a critical point

[2] See for example, Human Rights Watch (2022), Synovitz (2022) and Parker and Ilyushina (2022).

of contention for the state as the allegation of subservience to Russia undermines the very notion of sovereignty and independence that the "terrorists" were infringing upon. Tokayev several times stressed the limited nature of CSTO involvement and that no quid-pro-quo arrangement took place behind the scenes. The CSTO forces were there to guide units of critical infrastructure and were not engaging directly with the armed groups or the population. As soon as the situation "stabilized," they withdrew in full capacity. "As for the rumors that we supposedly owe something, there were no conversations with Putin - and there were many of them and they were all positive – regarding the fact that we would pay back later. And there were no prior conditions from the Kremlin either. At the end of the day, Russia is Kazakhstan's ally" (Transcript 8). In addition to refuting the rumors of a behind-the-scenes pact with Putin, Tokayev also tried to anchor the CSTO involvement in regional multilateralism by highlighting the input from other CSTO member states. "The very news of the arrival of the [CSTO] peacekeeping contingent in Kazakhstan played a very important role of psychological intimidation for the bandits. By the way, this was a joint peacekeeping contingent. In addition to Russia, there were military units from Belarus, Tajikistan, Armenia, and Kyrgyzstan." Tokayev also made a visible effort to signal that they won this battle over terrorists with their "own forces" (Transcript 12).

Finally, attempts at rebranding the January events and deleting tweets indicate the interactive and responsive nature of state framing. The violent turn of events with an unprecedented death toll led select activists to come up with the name "Qandy Qantar" or "Bloody January." This name has been picked up by civil society and the broader population, with appearances in foreign media. Tokayev's early speeches refrained from using this name and instead referred to "tragic events" or "tragic days" of January. By January 14, his Twitter introduced the term "Tragic January," which has since been the only way the government refers to the January events. In fact, a quick general search by the hashtag "#TragicJanuary" on Twitter will reveal that it has been predominantly used by state bodies like the Ministry of Foreign Affairs and embassies abroad. Such a strategy makes sense from the standpoint of blame attribution. While Bloody January stresses the violence of the event, Tragic January suggests a tragedy that happened to the nation of Kazakhstan. Such divergence of framing echoes a broader variation in blame attribution in major historical events in the region, including the framing of the mass death of a third of the ethnic Kazakh population in the

1930s as "famine" in Kazakhstan contrasted with a parallel framing in Ukraine of an agentic and even genocidal "*holodomor*" against Ukrainians despite both being product of the same Soviet policy of collectivization and industrialization (Richter, 2020).

The government also removed elements of the narrative that did not fit the new narrative. Multiple news outlets still have news of Tokayev informing the public over Twitter that at least 20 thousand terrorists participated in the Almaty attacks and that some of them "spoke non-Kazakh languages" (RBC News, 2022). However, the tweets were later deleted, likely after audience reactions to the plausibility of the claims in the absence of any hard evidence. Mediazona still features the screenshots of this deleted thread of Tokayev's tweets in English.[3] These tweets demonstrate attempts at bringing the audience on the same page with the state by appealing to the norm of the unacceptability of holding talks with terrorists, and portraying a horrifying picture on the ground to both deter people from going outside and justifying radical responses.

Conclusion: A New Kazakhstan?

During the events, Tokayev made frequent appeals to unity. "Together, as a single nation, we defended Almaty and other regional centers" (Transcript 5). Tokayev frequently framed himself as the person responsible for protecting the "safety and tranquility of our citizens" (Transcript 1). "In fact, this is no longer just a terrorist threat; this is an [attack] undermining of the integrity of the state, an attack on our citizens who ask me, as the Head of State, to urgently help them" (Transcript 1). "We will not allow encroachment on our state sovereignty and territorial integrity" (Transcript 4). Tokayev interprets the January unrest as an attack on the "sovereignty" and "territorial integrity" of Kazakhstan, an attack on *our* state and *our* citizens. Such framing seeks to prompt a sense of shared injustice and feeling of being wronged for all Kazakhstanis and puts the state and citizens on the same side by emphasizing the shared civic identity, contrasted by bandits and terrorists who arrived "from the outside" (Transcript 9). He lauded those who remained loyal:

[3] "Gangsters and terrorists [were] very well-trained, organized and commanded by the special centre. Some of them were speaking non-Kazakh languages. There were at least six waves of attacks of terrorists at Almaty, total amount of them 20 thousand" (January 8, twitter @TokayevKZ cited in Mediazona, 2022).

> Now I want to tell you, dear compatriots, that I am proud of you. I express my gratitude to those citizens of Kazakhstan who have kept calm these days and have made efforts to ensure stability and public order. Despite provocations and destructive appeals, you remained faithful to the law and your country. (Transcript 3)

Speaking to the nation on January 5, the worst day of violence, Tokayev was already striking an optimistic tone:

> Together we will overcome this black streak in the history of Kazakhstan. Let's come out of it strong. Soon I will come up with new proposals for the political transformation of Kazakhstan. I remain in the same position of consistent reforms. (Transcript 1)

On January 11, in an address in parliament on the events, Tokayev first mentioned the term "New Kazakhstan," stating that "together we will overcome all difficulties, together we will build a new Kazakhstan." Over the following months, this became a catchphrase of the regime, used to signify the changes the government proclaimed were happening in the country after the January events. In his address on March 16, Tokayev expanded on his vision for a New Kazakhstan. "We must learn important lessons from the January events," he stated. "The events of January shook the society," he continued. "Our people faced an unprecedented challenge, with the country's integrity under threat. During these days, we have deeply realized the lasting value of independence and how important peace, stability, and harmony are." Beyond reminding the population about the importance of stability, Tokayev blamed the January events on "domestic stagnation." Specifically, he argued that "an important lesson of the 'Tragic January' is that the concentration of power in the hands of the highest official in the state unnecessarily increases the influence of those close to him, as well as of financial and oligarchic groups. And they perceive the state as a personal fiefdom" (Transcript 12).

Based on this lesson, Tokayev argued that "systemic changes in all spheres of life" were necessary. Tokayev's planned "political transformation is aimed at forming fair and just "rules of the game," eradicating favoritism and monopolies in all spheres of life." He called on the government to build "A strong President – an influential Parliament – an accountable Government." The plan includes limiting presidential powers, strengthening parliament, and making it easier to register political parties.

Six months after Bloody January, the government proposed 56 amendments to the constitution. These included reducing the power of the senate, limiting the President to one seven-year term in office, reforming the constitutional court, and holding elections for local mayors (although the President chooses the candidates). The constitutional amendments passed a popular referendum with 77% of the vote on June 5, 2022.

Skepticism remains about how new the "New Kazakhstan" is and if the recent package of reforms will indeed improve governance, advance citizens' welfare, and democratize the political space. However, if it does indeed revert back to the top-down technocratic authoritarianism, it will now be under the new leadership of President Tokayev. The January events provided Tokayev with an opportunity to update and adjust the hegemonic narrative in a way that legitimizes the current administration. The largest nationwide crisis in the 30-year history of Kazakhstan as an independent state became a cut-off point for the government to differentiate and create distance between Nazarbayev's Old Kazakhstan and Tokayev's New.

Over the first few months of 2022 the state developed narrative frames to promote its version of what happened during the January events, to attribute blame for the mass violence, destruction, and loss of lives, to justify its radical and exceptional measures, and to reassert its role as the protector of the people. However, this strategic narrative did not end when the dust settled. Instead, it continues to serve as a legitimizing tool for the regime's longer-term objectives of strengthening control of the population.

Appendix: List of Transcripts

Transcript 1: "President Kassym-Jomart Tokayev addressed the people of Kazakhstan." Tengri TV. January 5, 2022.

https://www.youtube.com/watch?v=DgBQTH249y8&feature=youtu.be.

Transcript 2: "President Kassym-Jomart Tokayev's statement in regard to the current situation in the country." Press Service of the President of Kazakhstan. January 7, 2022.

https://www.youtube.com/watch?v=CzdXoEuUD5k.

Transcript 3: "President Kassym-Jomart Tokayev's address to the people of Kazakhstan." Press Service of the President of Kazakhstan. January 10, 2022.

https://www.youtube.com/watch?v=SdQOQpe5vBQ.

Transcript 4: "President Kassym-Jomart Tokayev's speech at an extraordinary session of the CSTO Collective Security Council." Press Service of the President of Kazakhstan. January 10, 2022.

https://www.youtube.com/watch?v=wIiJmgAR82E&t=4s.

Transcript 5: "President Kassym-Jomart Tokayev's speech at a meeting of the Majilis of the Parliament of the Republic of Kazakhstan." Press Service of the President of Kazakhstan. January 11, 2022.

https://www.youtube.com/watch?v=UuOKY791w60.

Transcript 6: "President Kassym-Jomart Tokayev held a meeting with representatives of domestic business." Press Service of the President of Kazakhstan. January 21, 2022.

https://www.youtube.com/watch?v=bhis_lJEv1I.

Transcript 7: "President K. Tokayev's speech at the Extraordinary XXI Congress of the Nur Otan Party." Press Service of the President of Kazakhstan. January 28, 2022.

https://www.youtube.com/watch?v=t9WKXfAidGw.

Transcript 8: "Exclusive interview of the President of the Republic of Kazakhstan Kassym-Jomart Tokayev to the Khabar Agency." Channel Khabar 24. January 29, 2022.

https://youtu.be/lwzhOH-xcgI.

Transcript 9: "President Kassym-Jomart Tokayev's address to the people of Kazakhstan." Press Service of the President of Kazakhstan. February 13, 2022.

https://www.youtube.com/watch?v=2VcjVtTuk_k.

Transcript 10: "Interview of President Kassym-Jomart Tokayev to the national TV channel 'Qazaqstan.'" Press Service of the President of Kazakhstan. February 17, 2022.

https://www.youtube.com/watch?v=pAJpWopjiKM.

Transcript 11: "Kasym-Jomart Tokayev's speech at an extraordinary meeting of the Council of Foreign Investors." Channel Khabar 24. February 23, 2022.

https://www.youtube.com/watch?v=uu3NLrz2jb0.

Transcript 12: "State address of the Head of State Kasym-Jomart Tokayev to the people of Kazakhstan. 'New Kazakhstan: The Path of

Renewal and Modernization.'" Press Service of the President of Kazakhstan. March 16, 2022.
https://www.youtube.com/watch?v=Nvs5RMQIYUo.

References

Adams, L. L., & Rustemova, A. (2009). Mass Spectacle and Styles of Governmentality in Kazakhstan and Uzbekistan. *Europe-Asia Studies, 61*(7), 1249–1276.

Aisarina, Z., Wilbur, E., Simpson, N., Kalmurzaeva, E., Meyer, J., Mutalov, D., & Ramazan Ali, H. (2021). *Covid-19, Worker Strikes and the Failure to Protect Citizens: An Update on the Central Asian Protest Tracker*. Oxus Society.

Akorda. (2019, September 2). *President of Kazakhstan Kassym-Jomart Tokaev's State of the Nation Address*. https://www.akorda.kz/en/addresses/addresses_of_president/president-of-kazakhstan-kassym-jomart-Tokaevs-state-of-the-nation-address-september-2-2019

Anceschi, L. (2022). The Week that Changed Kazakhstan Forever. *Open Democracy*. https://www.opendemocracy.net/en/odr/the-week-that-changed-kazakhstan-forever/

Askar, A. (2022). Kazakh-Russian Relations in the Context of the War in Ukraine. *The Diplomat*. https://thediplomat.com/2022/03/kazakh-russian-relations-in-the-context-of-the-war-in-ukraine/

BBC News. (2022, January 11). *Как события в казахстане повлияют на будущее россии и СНГ? Мнения политологов*. https://www.bbc.com/russian/features-59817255

Benford, R. D., & Snow, D. A. (2000). Framing Processes and Social Movements: An Overview and Assessment. *Annual Review of Sociology, 26*(1), 611–639.

Bishara, D. (2015). The Politics of Ignoring: Protest Dynamics in Late Mubarak Egypt. *Perspectives on Politics, 13*(4), 958–975.

Carey, S. C. (2010). The Use of Repression as a Response to Domestic Dissent. *Political Studies, 58*(1), 167–186.

Chang, P., & Vitale, A. (2013). Repressive Coverage in an Authoritarian Context: Threat, Weakness, and Legitimacy in South Korea's Democracy Movement. *Mobilization: An International Quarterly, 18*(1), 19–39.

CSTO. (2022). *Contingents of the CSTO Collective Peacekeeping Forces Are Deployed to the Republic of Kazakhstan*. https://en.odkb-csto.org/news/news_odkb/kontingenty-kollektivnykh-mirotvorcheskikh-sil-odkb-napravleny-v-respubliku-kazakhstan/#loaded

Davenport, C. (2005). *Repression and Mobilization*. University of Minnesota Press.

de Oliveira, R. S. (2011). Illiberal Peacebuilding in Angola. *The Journal of Modern African Studies, 49*(2), 287–314.
Dukalskis, A. (2017). *The Authoritarian Public Sphere Legitimation and Autocratic Power in North Korea, Burma, and China*. Routledge.
Dukalskis, A. (2021). *Making the World Safe for Dictatorship*. Oxford University Press.
Edel, M., & Josua, M. (2018). How Authoritarian Rulers Seek to Legitimize Repression: Framing Mass Killings in Egypt and Uzbekistan. *Democratization, 25*(5), 882–900.
Fairclough, N. (1992). *Discourse and Social Change*. Polity.
Fauve, A. (2015). Global Astana: Nation Branding as a Legitimization Tool for Authoritarian Regimes. *Central Asian Survey, 34*(1), 110–124.
Feldstein, S. (2022). Government Internet Shutdowns Are Changing. How Should Citizens and Democracies Respond? *Carnegie Endowment for International Peace*.
Ferree, M. M. (2003). Resonance and Radicalism: Feminist Framing in the Abortion Debates of the United States and Germany. *American Journal of Sociology, 109*(2), 304–344.
Foa, R. (2018). Modernization and Authoritarianism. *Journal of Democracy, 29*(3), 129–140.
Francisco, R. A. (2005). The Dictator's Dilemma. *Repression and mobilization, 64*(2), 58–81.
Freedom House. (2022). *Kazakhstan: Freedom House Urges De-escalation of Violence, Movement Toward Rule of Law*. https://freedomhouse.org/article/kazakhstan-freedom-house-urges-de-escalation-violence-movement-toward-rule-law
Gerschewski, J. (2013). The Three Pillars of Stability: Legitimation, Repression, and Co-optation in Autocratic Regimes. *Democratization, 20*(1), 13–38.
Gerschewski, J., & Dukalskis, A. (2017). What Autocracies Say (and What Citizens HEAR): Proposing Four Mechanisms of Autocratic Legitimation. *Contemporary Politics, 23*(3), 251–268.
Gohdes, A. R. (2020). Repression Technology: Internet Accessibility and State Violence. *American Journal of Political Science, 64*(3), 488–503.
Government of Kazakhstan. (2012). Law on National Security of the Republic of Kazakhstan. Available: https://adilet.zan.kz/eng/docs/Z1200000527
Gramsci, A. (1971). *Prison Notebooks:* (Vol. 1). Columbia University Press.
Gunitsky, S. (2015). Corrupting the Cyber-Commons: Social Media as a Tool of Autocratic Stability. *Perspectives on Politics, 13*(1), 42–54.
Guriev, S., & Treisman, D. (2019). Informational Autocrats. *Journal of Economic Perspectives, 33*(4), 100–127.

Heathershaw, J., & Mullojonov, P. (2018). (2018) Rebels without a Cause? Authoritarian Conflict Management in Tajikistan, 2008–2015. In M. Laruelle (Ed.), *Tajikistan on the Move* (pp. 33–62). Lexington.

Heathershaw, J., & Owen, C. (2019). Authoritarian Conflict Management in Post-colonial Eurasia. *Conflict, Security & Development, 19*(3), 269–273.

Human Rights Watch. (2022, January 11). *Kazakhstan: Cancel 'Shoot Without Warning' Order*. Human Rights Watch. https://www.hrw.org/news/2022/01/07/kazakhstan-cancel-shoot-without-warning-order

Ilyushina, M., & Cheng A. (2022) Kazakhstan President Gives Shoot-To-Kill Order Against Protesters, Dismissing Calls for Negotiations. *Washington Post.*

Insebayeva, S., & Insebayeva, N. (2021). The Power of Ambiguity: National Symbols, Nation-Building and Political Legitimacy in Kazakhstan. *Europe-Asia Studies, 74*(4), 660–682.

Johnston, H. (2005). Talking the Walk: Speech Acts and Resistance in Authoritarian Regimes. *Repression and Mobilization, 21*, 108–137.

Karibayeva, A., & Meyer, J. (2022). *Kazakhstan's Reforms Should Be More Than Just Show*. Foreign Policy.

Keremoğlu, E., & Weidmann, N. B. (2020). How Dictators Control the Internet: A Review Essay. *Comparative Political Studies, 53*(10–11), 1690–1703.

Koopmans, R. (2005). Repression and the Public Sphere: Discursive Opportunities for Repression Against the Extreme Right in Germany in the 1990s. *Repression and Mobilization, 21*, 58–81.

Kucera, J. (2022). *CSTO Agrees to Intervene in Kazakhstan Unrest*. https://eurasianet.org/csto-agrees-to-intervene-in-kazakhstan-unrest

Larson, J. (2019). Collective Action in the Information Age: How Social Media Shapes the Character and Success of Protests. In M. Arce & R. Rice (Eds.), *Protest and Democracy* (pp. 71–92). University of Calgary Press.

Lewis, D. (2016). Blogging Zhanaozen: Hegemonic Discourse and Authoritarian Resilience in Kazakhstan. *Central Asian Survey, 35*(3), 421–438.

Lewis, D., Heathershaw, J., & Megoran, N. (2018). Illiberal Peace? Authoritarian Modes of Conflict Management. *Cooperation and Conflict, 53*(4), 486–506.

Marat, E. (2016). Post-violence Regime Survival and Expansion in Kazakhstan and Tajikistan. *Central Asian Survey, 35*(4), 531–548.

Mayer, R. (2001). Strategies of Justification in Authoritarian Ideology. *Journal of Political Ideologies, 6*(2), 147–168.

Mediazona. (2022). *Tokayev Deleted Tweets About 6 Waves of Attempts to Seize Almaty*. https://mediazona.ca/news/2022/01/08/udoli

Megoran, N. (2008). Framing Andijon, Narrating the Nation: Islam Karimov's Account of the Events of 13 May 2005. *Central Asian Survey, 27*(1), 15–31.

MK. (2022). *Media: In Return for Help, Russia Demands Kazakhstan to Recognize Crimea*. https://www.mk.ru/politics/2022/01/06/smi-rossiya-v-obmen-na-pomoshh-kazakhstanu-trebuet-priznat-krym.html

Morgenbesser, L. (2020). The Menu of Autocratic Innovation. *Democratization, 27*(6), 1053–1072.

Omelicheva, M. Y. (2016). Authoritarian Legitimation: Assessing Discourses of Legitimacy in Kazakhstan and Uzbekistan. *Central Asian Survey, 35*(4), 481–500.

Orisbayev, Z. (2022). *Food and Cash Shortages Spread as Kazakhstan Throttles Internet*. https://eurasianet.org/food-and-cash-shortages-spread-as-kazakhstan-throttles-internet

Owen, C., Juraev, S., Heathershaw, J., Lewis, D., & Megoran, N. (2018). *Interrogating Illiberal Peace in Eurasia Critical Perspectives on Peace and Conflict*. Rowan & Littlefield.

Parker, C., & Ilyushina, M. (2022, January 11). Why Is Kazakhstan Claiming Foreign Links to the Unrest? Here's What We Know. *Washington Post*. https://www.washingtonpost.com/world/2022/01/08/kazakhstan-foreign-protests/

Rampton, D. (2011). 'Deeper Hegemony': The Politics of Sinhala Nationalist Authenticity and the Failures of Power-Sharing in Sri Lanka. *Commonwealth & Comparative Politics, 49*(2), 245–273.

RBC News. (2022b). *Tokayev on Almaty Attackers Who Spoke Non-Kazakh Languages*. https://www.rbc.ru/politics/07/01/2022/61d89de99a7947e67a6c2491

Richter, J. (2020). Famine, Memory, and Politics in the Post-Soviet Space: Contrasting Echoes of Collectivization in Ukraine and Kazakhstan. *Nationalities papers, 48*(3), 476–491.

Schatz, E. (2009). The Soft Authoritarian Tool Kit: Agenda-Setting Power in Kazakhstan and Kyrgyzstan. *Comparative Politics, 41*(2), 203–222.

Schatz, E., & Maltseva, E. (2012). Kazakhstan's Authoritarian "Persuasion." *Post-Soviet Affairs, 28*(1), 45–65.

Smith, C. Q., Waldorf, L., Venugopal, R., & McCarthy, G. (2020). Illiberal Peace-Building in Asia: A Comparative Overview. *Conflict, Security & Development, 20*(1), 1–14.

Sutton, J., Butcher, C. R., & Svensson, I. (2014). Explaining Political jiu-jitsu: Institution-Building and the Outcomes of Regime Violence Against Unarmed Protests. *Journal of Peace Research, 51*(5), 559–573.

Synovitz, R. (2022, January 7). *'We Are Not Terrorists!': Kazakh Protesters Try to Make Their Voices Heard Amid the Chaos*. RFE/RL. https://www.rferl.org/a/kazakhstan-voices-protesters-complaints-tokayev/31644144.html

Tilly, C. (2003). *The Politics of Collective Violence*. Cambridge University Press.

Torfing, J. (1999). *New Theories of Discourse: Laclau, Mouffe and Zizek*. Wiley-Blackwell.

Tufekci, Z., & Wilson, C. (2012). Social Media and the Decision to Participate in Political Protest: Observations from Tahrir Square. *Journal of Communication, 62*(2), 363–379.

Valiyev, A., & Valiyev, A. (2015). Urban Boosterism in Closed Contexts: Spectacular Urbanization and Second-tier Mega-Events in Three Caspian Capitals. *Eurasian Geography and Economics, 56*(5), 575–598. https://doi.org/10.1080/15387216.2016.1146621

van Dijk, T. A. (1993). Principles of Critical Discourse Analysis. *Discourse & Society, 4*(2), 249–283.

von Soest, C., & Grauvogel, J. (2015). *How Do Non-Democratic Regimes Claim Legitimacy?: Comparative Insights from Post-Soviet Countries*. German Institute of Global and Area Studies (GIGA).

Woodhams, S., & Migliano, S. (2022). *Government Internet Shutdowns Have Cost Over $21 Billion Since 2019*. https://www.top10vpn.com/research/cost-of-internet-shutdowns/

Zhao, D. (2009). The Mandate of Heaven and Performance Legitimation in Historical and Contemporary China. *American Behavioral Scientist, 53*(3), 416–433.

Foreign Terrorists and Kyrgyz Jazzmen: Framing the January 2022 Unrest in Kazakhstan

Hélène Thibault and Nurmakhan Tastaibek

Abstract This chapter looks at the reasons why the Kazakhstani state authorities blamed the January 2022 violence on foreign-trained terrorists. We argue that the authorities shifted the blame to foreign elements for three reasons related to both internal and external legitimation purposes. First, we demonstrate that invoking the Islamic rhetoric represents a typical tactic used by the Kazakhstani government to delegitimize opposition movements. Second, shifting away the blame from the population allows the authorities to minimize and to some extent write off the profound underlying popular discontent. Third, we argue that invoking the presence of "foreign agents" in the unrest was a necessary condition for the involvement of the Collective Security Treaty Organization (CSTO) forces.

H. Thibault (✉) · N. Tastaibek
Nazarbayev University, Astana, Kazakhstan
e-mail: helene.thibault@nu.edu.kz

N. Tastaibek
e-mail: nurmakhan.tastaibek@nu.edu.kz

J.-F. Caron (ed.), *A Revolt in the Steppe*, The Steppe and Beyond: Studies on Central Asia,
https://doi.org/10.1007/978-981-99-0783-0_5

Keywords Securitization · Authoritarianism · Kazakhstan · Legitimation · Terrorism · Protests

Introduction

"They said that Kazakhs were not the kind of people to take the streets, that they were well behaved, cautious and resilient, but us, we are tired, we can't take it anymore."[1] This is how a middle-aged man who participated in protests in Almaty described people's involvement in the mass unrest that shook the country in January 2022. The protests which started in the Western city of Aktau, located by the Caspian Sea, rapidly spread all over Kazakhstan and took indeed a lot of observers by surprise. Unlike some of its neighbors, notably Kyrgyzstan which has seen three government overthrows since 2005, Kazakhstan was considered a very stable, soft authoritarian regime where the standards of living are notably higher than its post-Soviet neighbors. That is not to say that protests did not take place prior to that. In Zhanaozen, another Western city, oil workers organized protests due to the socio-economic problems in the region in 2011. Protests turned deadly when security forces tried to disperse the workers, an intervention that resulted in the death of 14 protesters (Satpayev & Umbetaliyeva, 2015). Other major protests followed the government's announcement of a land privatization policy in 2016 and the appointment of the successor of the first President of Kazakhstan in 2019 (Caron & Malikova, 2021; Heuer & Hierman, 2022). However, the scale and the violence of the January mobilization took many by surprise, including the authorities, and shook the regime's foundations. It is not simple to make sense of this popular mobilization that also happened against the backdrop of intense elite competition and rumors of a failed coup. Kudaibergenova and Laruelle (2022) mention that opposing groups within the elite might have used a disagreement in demands and a lack of organized mobilization of protestors to orchestrate a coup against President Kassym-Jomart Tokayev. Tokayev, sidelining his predecessor and detaining people related to him, like intelligence head

[1] https://pages.rts.ch/emissions/geopolitis/12748944-kazakhstan-revolte-matee.html.

Karim Massimov, in the aftermath of the January events, begs a question if they were behind the alleged coup. However, our intention here is not to uncover the details of these events but to analyze how the authorities have framed the protests. Indeed, the authorities were quick to blame foreign elements for the unrest and President Tokayev tweeted: "The analysis of the situation showed that Kazakhstan is facing an armed act of aggression well prepared and coordinated by perpetrators and terrorist groups trained outside the country."[2] However, authorities did not provide serious evidence to substantiate those accusations, and a ludicrous news story about an alleged paid mercenary who turned out to be a Kyrgyz jazzman whom the authorities forced into confession, shattered those claims.[3]

The President's interpretation of the riots comforts the opinion that indeed, ordinary Kazakhs could not have been responsible for that unrest. His statement also contradicts the existent literature that posits Kazakhstan as a country mostly inimical to Islamic radicalization (Montgomery & Heathershaw, 2016; Omelicheva, 2011; Thibault, 2019). This chapter will look at how the concept of Islamic radicalization was used as a political instrument in addressing the January events in Kazakhstan and argue that the authorities shifted the blame to foreign elements for three reasons related to both internal and external legitimation purposes. First, we demonstrate that invoking the Islamic rhetoric represents a typical tactic used by Central Asian governments to delegitimize opposition movements. Second, shifting away the blame from the population allows the authorities to minimize and to some extent write off the profound underlying popular discontent. Third, we argue that invoking the presence of "foreign agents" in the unrest was a necessary condition for the involvement of the Collective Security Treaty Organization (CSTO) forces.

Framing the January Violence

Protests started in Zhanaozen on January 2, 2022. Residents first complained about the increase in the price of liquefied petroleum gas,

[2] https://www.washingtonpost.com/world/2022/01/08/kazakhstan-foreign-protests/.

[3] https://www.youtube.com/watch?v=6YYhOAvhOm0.

the fuel of choice in the region. However, as the protests spread quickly throughout Kazakhstan, additional demands were adopted—mainly eradicating former President Nazarbayev's hold over Kazakhstan's political and economic spheres.[4] Nursultan Nazarbayev ruled the country for thirty years until he voluntarily left his position in 2019. Tokayev who was then Speaker of the Senate, became interim President as stated by the Kazakhstani constitution until he was elected in snap election in June 2019. Although Tokayev has been the head of state and of the executive since then, Nazarbayev maintained major positions such as the head of the ruling party, Nur-Otan (renamed Amanat in March 2022), and head of the Security Council, a powerful executive organ. On January 4 in Almaty, thousands marched peacefully until demonstrations got out of control and were followed by unrest. A protestor mentioned: "30,000 people were just walking peacefully towards the New Square. I believe that all these protests were swayed by provocateurs" (Turgayev, 2022, para. 12). There are no official data on the number of protesters, but Zhursyn (2022, para. 10) indicates that protests in Almaty, Aktau, and Zhanaozen on January 5 may have gathered up to 10,000 people. Protests in Aktau and Zhanaozen, like in many other cities, were solely peaceful. Nevertheless, the peaceful protests in Almaty turned into riots, including arson of government buildings and looting; residences of the President and the akimat (mayor's office) were burned down; the protesters even seized the Almaty airport. The authorities lost control over the city. As a result of the January events, 225 people died across Kazakhstan, and 4,353 were injured, most of them in Almaty.[5] Material damage to state buildings and private properties was also colossal and amounted to 92.8 billion tenge (approximately 190 million USD).[6]

Tokayev claimed, on January 10 that "more than 20,000 "bandits," "terrorists" and "extremists" invaded and ransacked Almaty in a preplanned attempt to execute a coup" (Oxford Analytica, 2022, para. 9). However, there was no significant evidence to support his claim, which potentially leaves to think that the threat of Islamic radicalization was instrumentalized to legitimize the government's response. Moreover,

[4] https://www.ft.com/content/90355e64-c3bb-43ee-bec4-37e3e2c70a60.

[5] https://www.youtube.com/watch?v=LPExUBjjqPw.

[6] http://ranking.kz/ru/a/infopovody/materialnyj-usherb-ot-ugolovnyh-pravonarushenij-uvelichilsya-srazu-na-68-za-god.

after the police started a "witch hunting" of non-Caucasian foreigners, the national TV channel, Khabar-24, broadcasted a special program on funding the alleged foreign fighters.[7] The channel aired a confession of a Kyrgyz citizen who claimed to have been paid 200 US dollars to ransack the streets of Almaty. However, the Kyrgyz government issued a note to Kazakhstan after its citizens recognized him as a famous Jazz player.[8] After the police released him, he confessed to admitting an alleged criminal act under torture. In the next section, we look into how the government tried to blame Islamic radicals but we argue that these claims were not credible and were formulated in order to remove the burden of guilt from the population, which also represents a way to undermine people's grievances and avoid recognizing the government's inadequacies.

The Islamic Threat

Since the early days of independence, numerous scholars and observers have written about the "Islamic threat" in Central Asia, suggesting that local Muslim communities could fall under the influence of foreign radical Islamic groups or, since the rise of Taliban, be victims of an Afghan spillover (Malashenko, 1994; Matveeva, 2018; Naumkin, 2005). Yet, history has mostly proven them wrong, and a large proportion of the literature on the region suggests that Islamic radicalization has been highly exaggerated, could even be considered a myth, and that governments use it as a political instrument to restrict the opposition, gain political legitimacy and prevent active mobilization (Montgomery & Heathershaw, 2016; Lemon & Thibault, 2018; Omelicheva, 2011). But why Islamic radicalism?

In Kazakhstan, Islam is now the dominant religion after the demographic balance shifted in favor of "ethnic Kazakhs" who were a minority in Soviet times. In the latest census conducted in 2021, 69.31% of the population mentioned Islam as their religious affiliation (Biuro natsionalnoi statistiki Agentstva po strategicheskomu planirovaniyu i reformam Respubliki Kazakhstan, 2022). However, the state and the population

[7] https://kloop.kg/blog/2022/01/09/kyrgyzskogo-dzhazovogo-muzykanta-v-kazahstane-pytayutsya-vydat-za-uchastnika-pogromov/.

[8] https://www.bbc.com/russian/features-59911453.

are resolutely secular. Secularization already started under Russian imperialism when society shifted from Sharia-associated laws and norms to secular laws as the Russian Empire penetrated Kazakh society. Kazakh intellectuals of the Tsarist period such as Dulat Babatayuli and Shortanbay Qanayuly, complained about life under the Russian laws and believed they negatively impacted the Islamic faith. For example, Shortanbay shared his dissatisfaction with Kazakhs adhering to imperial laws and sending their children to religious institutions (Uyama, 2013).

Soviet colonization furthered secularization: the Communist Party did not welcome the practice of religion and instead promoted atheism. Sovietologists argue that state officials depicted Islam negatively, Islam was not only a religious belief that comforted uneducated people but also had a destabilizing potential (Thibault, 2022). In that regard, Moscow regulated Islam through the Committee for Religious Affairs, which served to sanction and establish religious institutions and report on the religious situation since 1918, and through the Spiritual Direction of Muslims of Central Asia with the jurisdiction to appoint religious personnel since 1943 (Thibault, 2019). The latter organization transformed into the Spiritual Direction of Muslims in Kazakhstan (SDMK), continuing the Soviet legacy of secularism and regulation. However, a perestroika-era and then post-Soviet phenomenon have influenced the expansion of Islam in people's lives (Montgomery & Heathershaw, 2016) and Kazakhstan has been experiencing a moderate religious revival. The revival is constituted by incremental "Islamization" of Kazakhstan and growth in individual piety and public expressions of Islam. One third of people identifying as Muslims fast during the holy month of Ramadan (Malik, 2019) and the popularity of Islamic pilgrimages: 228 people went to Mecca (the holy city of Muslims) in 2001 versus 3000 people in 2018. The number of mosques increased from 68 in 1991 to 2516 in 2016 (Malik, 2019). Although the practice of Islam is not homogeneous, the revival is especially seen among conservative Sunni traditionalists, deriving from the increasing popularity and consolidation of conservative Sunni Islam (Zhussipbek et al., 2020). The influence of conservative Islam was demonstrated during the COVID-19 quarantine when one of the well-known poets recognized for defending conservative Islamic principles received an award by the ruling party despite his public disbelief in COVID-19. Also, the funeral of another notable Muslim figure was attended by thousands of people while rigid quarantine restrictions were on the ground and the police did not manage to disperse his followers

(Zhussipbek et al., 2020). These factors indicate that Kazakhstan is experiencing a moderate Islamic revival. However, "Islamization" does not necessarily lead to radicalization.

Omelicheva (2011) suggests that the participation of Kazakhstani citizens in extremist activities is limited and unlikely due to the persistence of secular values which posits Kazakhstan as a country inimical to extremist and terrorist activities whether it is within or outside the state. However, authorities are very keen to emphasize the threat of radical Islam (Thibault, 2020; 2022). Montgomery and Heathershaw (2016) reach similar conclusions and argue that the relationship between Islamization and radicalization is problematic and practically impossible to evaluate. Also, the authors underline that among the few cases of confirmed terrorist attacks perpetrated by Islamic radicals, none of them had connections with foreign organizations. Yet, these studies were published before it became known that the Islamic State in Syria (ISIS) managed to attract recruits from Central Asia.

Although Central Asia remains outside the scope of ISIS's physical presence, recruits from the former Soviet Union republics outnumbered that from any other regions between 2012 and 2015 (Thibault, 2018; Tucker, 2018). Interestingly, recruitment appears to bear a specific regional character. For Kyrgyzstan and Tajikistan, a disproportionate number of recruits were from the Aravan district and Khatlon province, respectively, while for Kazakhstan, the urban areas of Zhezkazgan, Atyrau, and Aktobe were of particular concern. What connects these cities is the seclusion and extraction of underground resources and Tucker (2018) argues that the inequality in these areas might cause extremist arguments to resonate with possible recruits. Although it poses a legitimate concern, Kazakhstan is highly secular and there is little evidence proving that locally radicalized Kazakhstanis have connections to transnational organizations.

The 9/11 terrorist attack on the United States created hype around Islamic terrorism, gathering the world's sympathy and making them acknowledge the threats of Islamic radicalization. As a result, the United States started "The Global War on Terrorism" (GWOT), also known as the "war on terror," to justify its interventions in other sovereign states like Iran and Afghanistan. Since the US's influence in the international arena is significant, GWOT became a trend, enabling other states, including Kazakhstan, to utilize the GWOT for various political purposes. Despite its active stance against Islamic extremism, Kazakhstan, in particular, is not greatly affected by that and extremist migration from

Kazakhstan to areas of conflict. As of 2021, the Global Terrorism Index of Kazakhstan (GTI) is of zero,[9] indicating a lack of terror attacks within the state in the last five years. As of 2018, only 500–600 fighters joined jihadist groups in Syria and Iraq out of 5.500 fighters from Central Asia (Soliev, 2019). Moreover, Cammett and Jones (2022) reported that many of those who left to fight for terrorist organizations from Central Asia have been recruited from Russia during labor migration. It leaves little room for supporting the narrative around an increasing Islamic radicalization in Kazakhstan. It remains quite puzzling that Kazakhstan nationals were eager to join a fight that is so disconnected from their own reality given that so few have connections to the Middle Easter countries and speak Arabic and that so few of those radicals are active *within* Kazakhstan.

Yet, despite its limited reach, we cannot argue that Kazakhstan is not affected by Islamic radicalization. The singularity however is that contrary to what the authorities claim, domestic radicals are not necessarily connected to international actors. In 2016, Aktobe faced a terrorist attack by a group of individuals. It resulted in the deaths of dozens of people. Likewise, a terrorist attack in Almaty was executed in the same year. The attack has also led to victims' deaths, setting a red level of terrorist threat in Almaty. The state authority proclaimed that the members of both groups had non-traditional religious leanings, thus, connecting the incidents to Islam. We need to compare the two cases to analyze the extent of religious threats they posed to Kazakhstani citizens. Sharipova and Beissembayev (2021) mention that both attacks were clearly directed against law-enforcement institutions. After conducting interviews with the sentenced terrorists, they asserted that criminal youth subculture, grievances, and the Salafi-jihadist ideology were the reasons to motivate the criminals. Although the authors recognize the influence of Salafi-jihadist ideologies, they mention that social factors like poverty, unemployment, and social exclusion were causes of these acts no less than religious ideologies. Moreover, there was no evidence that these individuals had links to translational terrorist organizations.

Religious terrorism is a complex phenomenon of violent acts carried out by individuals or organizations to produce an environment of fear. "One implicit assumption is that the act is meant to affect a much larger

[9] https://www.visionofhumanity.org/maps/global-terrorism-index/#/.

audience in a given population, an audience in whom the act generates fear" (Corsi, 1981, p. 48). Contrary to the assumption, the people involved in Kazakhstani violent acts directed their anger not at citizens to create fear but at the law-enforcement institutions. Sharipova and Beissembayev (2021) discovered that criminals of these attacks encountered poverty and personal difficulties. Feelings of injustice were also present among convicts. Considering that the most radical extremists represent lower social strata in Central Asia, we can induce that the weight of social factors had a stronger influence on the occurrence of these acts rather than Islamic radicalization. Then why did state authorities blame Islamic radicalism to be the main cause of the terrorist attacks?

Montgomery and Heathershaw (2016) and Sailaubekuly (2019) suggest that, although there is widespread rhetoric on Islamic radicalism, there is not enough evidence to support the claim. They examined claims about Islam in Central Asia and showed how state officials seek to link all political opposition with Islamic radicalization. For example, Uzbekistan's former President used anti-terrorist rhetoric to justify his reaction to the Andijon events in 2005 (Montgomery & Heathershaw, 2016). The Tajik government also accused its main political opponent—the Islamic Revival Party of Tajikistan (IRPT)—of extremism and the Party was added to the list of extremist organizations in 2015 despite very dubious evidence (Thibault, 2018). The accusation of terrorism were rather part of a long-term strategy to annihilate the country's most organized opposition party. Although Kazakhstan does not directly link Islamic radicalism to political opposition, the government adopted extremist laws to combat Islamic radicalism that are then used to oppress political opponents and their followers. The Democratic Choice of Kazakhstan (DCK) was declared an extremist organization in 2018 despite being recognized as a peaceful opposition movement by the EU Parliament[10] (Reshetnyak & Omelicheva, 2022). Central Asian governments use the myth of Islamic radicalism as a foundation for restricting the activity of the opposition, a tactic that allows them to avoid international criticism and even get support from Western states (Montgomery & Heathershaw, 2016).

Drawing on the January events, it is unlikely that Islamic radicalization was the cause of the violence that spread in Kazakhstan due to the lack of evidence to back up state officials' claims. The lack of reliable and credible

[10] https://www.europarl.europa.eu/doceo/document/RC-9-2022-0065_EN.html.

evidence is complemented by inconsistency in officials' statements and the torture of suspects present in the aftermath of the unrest. President Tokayev tweeted that he would invite international organizations to investigate the causes and reactions to the events but later altered his mind and claimed it was unnecessary to invite foreign investigators as Kazakhstan has the capacity to conduct it itself. In his interview with the Khabar TV channel, he commented: "As for the international investigation into the events in Kazakhstan, I do not consider it necessary to conduct such an investigation. We can handle it ourselves; we have people who are honest and objective" (Radio Azattyq, 2022, para. 4). Yet, Kazakhstani officials did not produce any trustworthy evidence of the investigation to indicate the influence of Islamic extremism.

Moreover, Berik Asylov, Prosecutor General, answered a journalist's question about foreign fighters in the following way: "There were 19 foreigners among those detained in January - these are citizens of Russia, Uzbekistan, and Kyrgyzstan. In fact, they are all participants in the riots. There weren't 20 thousand foreign terrorists. I do not know where you got it" (Karina, 2022, para. 2). Asylov denied the existence of these people and seemed surprised to learn the numbers, despite President Tokayev tweeting about 20,000 "bandits," "terrorists," and "extremists." Even wilder claims were made by the President who accused terrorists of raiding Almaty's morgues and stealing the bodies of their dead accomplices. The President argued the latter was the practice of "international terrorists of known origin" to cover their tracks (CSTO, 2022).

On the other hand, there is the factor of torture. After broadcasting the Kyrgyz jazzman who confessed to being a paid mercenary under torture, state officials did not present any viable figures of the presence or arrest of foreign fighters. Even if such figures appear, it would be easy to question the credibility of those accusations due to the numerous cases of torture cases that were reported. By March 13, 2022, the Prosecutor General's Office confirmed 243 cases of torture of people captured during and after the January 2022 events (Vlast, 2022). It reveals that torture was widespread in the aftermath of the events, which makes us doubt even the credibility of people's confessions to looting. These actions conform to typical authoritarian repressive practices aimed at imposing order through coercion. However, the use of force is, for obvious reasons, highly unpopular and authoritarian governments can rely on it only temporarily, at the risk of antagonizing a too large portion of the population. Authoritarian regimes also need to maintain their legitimacy by controlling the information and framing the narratives in their favor.

Domestic and International Legitimacy Compromised

The government of Kazakhstan has a long history of censorship and manipulation of information (Lewis, 2016). Schatz for instance, demonstrated how the Kazakhstani authorities mastered the art of not only censoring information but "staging of political dramas that undermine opponents' efforts to gain popular support," a strategy he calls discursive preemption (Schatz, 2009, p. 207). Similarly, Sagadiyeva (2021) showed how public discussions concerning unpopular projects such as the legalization of polygyny were initiated to divert the public from more controversial issues which involved Nursultan Nazarbayev's son-in-law, Rakhat Aliyev. Finally, Lewis (2016) has shown how the regime, facing one of its earlier most severe crisis, the oil workers' strike in Zhanaozen in 2011, was able to circulate its hegemonic discourses through the use of seemingly independent bloggers, to present the role of authorities as guarantors of civil order fighting destructive elements. However, in the recent years, the Kazakhstani government has also relied on a different strategy to control information—to cut all access to it.

It has become routine for state authorities to temporarily disable access to social media (YouTube, Facebook, VKontake, Instagram) during live broadcasts of opposition leader in exile Mukhtar Ablyazov (Kumenov, 2018). It was also widely used during the protests that followed the 2019 early Presidential election when Tokayev became President (Caron & Malikova, 2021). Whereas it used to be an unofficial practice that the authorities never openly admitted, blocking Internet access is on its way to become sanctioned by law.[11] The control of the Internet was "necessary" and so was framing the narratives during the January events to avoid discrediting the government's actions toward protesters. Already on the first day of protests on January 2, the authorities started restricting

[11] https://www.rferl.org/a/kazakhstan-block-social-networks/31461720.html.

Internet access. As protests spread, access to Internet became more uncertain and ended in a complete, nationwide blackout on January 5, which lasted until January 10.[12]

Left in the dark, citizens, especially those living in areas where were no protests, had a limited understanding of what was truly happening. Apart from preventing the population from witnessing the violent events that were unfolding, we see in the Kazakhstani government's attitude, a willingness to shelter the population from blame. Tokayev rejected calls from abroad to hold talks with protesters to find a peaceful resolution: His response was: "What idiocy! What kind of negotiations can there be with criminals, murderers? We have had to deal with armed and trained bandits, both local and foreign" (Lillis, 2022a). This affirmation moves away the blame from ordinary citizens to marginal subgroups whose objective was to destabilize the country. Just like in Zhanaozen in 2011, the state narrative constructed an "external, illegitimate 'they' – contrasted to an internal, unified 'we'," which justified the use of brutal force (Lewis, 2016, p. 432). More than a benevolent attitude toward the general public, the government's refusal to acknowledge the grassroots character of the protests is in fact a way for the authorities to undermine peoples' grievances and avoid taking responsibility for its own inadequacies in satisfying people's economic and social needs.

The experience of such unprecedented violence that led to human losses and destruction could signal the regime's failure to provide satisfactory economic conditions and a safe social environment. If officials had acknowledged that the January 2022 events resulted from their own mismanagement and policy failures, they would have important introspection work to do. Thus, saying that the tragic events came as a product of some foreign forces' intervention would lessen the burden on the government, increasing their political legitimacy after the January 2022 events.

Conveniently, criminal laws on extremism and terrorism have vague wording, and it enables the government to use them to restrict criticism and opposition (Baisagatovaa et al., 2016). In 2015, 350 web pages were blocked by the Committee for Religious Affairs under the Ministry of Culture and Sports (Aaronson, 2017). In 2014, the laws allowed the Ministry to declare an organization terrorist (Stronski, 2016). In 2018, an

[12] For a detailed account of Internet shutdown, see https://www.accessnow.org/kazakhstan-internet-shutdowns-protests-almaty-timeline-whats-happening/.

unregistered oppositional party, DCK, was recognized as a terrorist organization. The laws' vague wording permitted the Committee and Ministry to monitor and block websites they deem extremist and declare them terrorist without the courts' approval. International organizations like Amnesty International consider these cases of restriction a violation of the freedom of speech. However, the government benefits from restricting the freedom of speech online and recognizing opposition as terrorists as criticism lowers its political legitimacy. Legitimacy focuses on the sphere of influence of political bodies and regimes. Since criticism questions the efficacy of such bodies and the regime, it also questions whether the regime should have a right to influence various spheres. Thus, the Kazakhstani political regime finds it justifiable to use the concept of Islamic radicalization to gain political legitimacy by restricting the opposition and criticism in general.

Kazakhstan's international legitimacy was also undermined by the massive violence and crackdown. In particular, the "shoot-to-kill without warning" order pronounced by Tokayev on January 7, prompted foreign governments and human rights organizations to denounce the Kazakhstani government's response.[13] By appealing to the CSTO, the government of Kazakhstan not only sought gunpower backup to quell demonstrations and looters, but also to legitimize its actions and share the burden of responsibility. The literature on regional authoritarian solidarity suggests that like-minded regimes enjoy extra legitimacy if these efforts take place within the framework of a regional organization (Libman & Obydenkova, 2018). None of the CSTO members can be counted as democracies and the infringement of human rights is likely to be ignored or even tolerated. However, it should be mentioned that CSTO forces on the ground did not interacted with civilian actors and their role was limited to protecting government structures and other buildings of strategic importance. As we discuss in the next section, the CSTO's first ever peace-making mission was significant for both the organization and for Kazakhstan.

[13] https://www.hrw.org/news/2022/01/07/kazakhstan-cancel-shoot-without-warning-order.

The Collective Security Treaty Organization's Intervention

As mentioned earlier, the Kazakhstani government did not manage to contain the unrest in Almaty: the army, police forces, and National Security Committee (NSC) could not handle the looting and execute orders on January 4–5. We distinguish two potential reasons behind the failure of law enforcement bodies. One is the performance and reliability of the NSC. President Tokayev, in his assessment of the government's reaction, mentioned, "Not everyone showed loyalty to their duty. In a number of cities, the heads of the departments of the National Security Committee, despite having a sufficient military arsenal, left the service buildings without engaging in battle, leaving weapons and secret documents there" (BBC News, 2022, para. 16). As a result, the head of NSC, Karim Massimov was taken to court for treason. Another possible reason might be the tactics of violent groups. Kudaibergenova and Laruelle (2022) argue that these groups were organized, struck those who attempted to capture their faces on camera, damaged surveillance cameras, and removed plates from their cars not to be identified. They wore regular garments that did not distinguish them from the remaining protestors and general citizens, which may have complicated the effectiveness of law enforcement.

The unrest and failure of law enforcement posited serious threats to the continuation of the current political regime. It spread all over Kazakhstan, and further escalation of violence would have delegitimized the authorities if it had come to a point that the population's safety was compromised and, if not, an overthrow of the regime. Thus, it was rational for President Tokayev to ask for external assistance. He requested military support from the Collective Security Treaty Organization (CSTO), to which it is a member, to intervene and ensure the survival of the current political regime.

The Collective Security Treaty Organization (CSTO) was established in 1992 with nine post-Soviet member states. Becoming a member state requires signing international treaties and resolutions with a further condition to renew the membership every five years. Three states decided to not to renew their membership in 1997: Uzbekistan, Georgia, and Azerbaijan. The organization currently comprises of six members: the Russian Federation, Belarus, Kazakhstan, Kyrgyzstan, Tajikistan, and

Armenia. Article 4 of the Collective Security Treaty (1992, para. 10) indicates:

> In case of aggression commission (armed attack menacing to safety, stability, territorial integrity and sovereignty) to any of the Member States, all the other Member States at request of this Member State shall immediately provide the latter with the necessary help, including military one, as well as provide support by the means at their disposal in accordance with the right to collective defense pursuant to article 51 of the UN Charter.

Article 4's verbatim does not explicitly refers to *foreign* or *external* aggression but it is interpreted as such. In June 2010, when Kyrgyzstan required the assistance of the CSTO to quell violent clashes between Uzbek and Kyrgyz communities in the south of the country, the CSTO refused to get involved. In particular, President Dimitry Medvedev mentioned that "Only in the case of a foreign intrusion and an attempt to externally seize power can we state that there is an attack against the CSTO" (Elder, 2010).[14] Kazakhstan was the first member state to employ the article: no military forces were deployed within the CSTO from the signing of the treaty until the January events. Nur-Sultan (renamed Astana in September 2022) claimed external terrorist threats were menacing its safety under Article 4 (Collective Security Treaty Organization, 2022). This claim was necessary to deploy foreign military forces. Considering there was hardly any reliable evidence of foreign intervention, it can be induced that the rhetoric of "foreign agents" was only used for the involvement of CSTO.

Yet, there were also incentives for the member states, especially Russia, to participate. Russia was on the eve of invading Ukraine and certainly needed to boost its region capital before that. Whereas Russia was often seen as the aggressor because of its involvement in Georgia and Crimea, by getting involved in restoring order Kazakhstan, it could now present itself as a peacemaker. Russia also sent a powerful message. Referring to the CSTO's first *and* successful mission, President Vladimir Putin mentioned that "The measures taken through the CSTO have clearly shown that we will not allow the situation to be shaken at home and

[14] The CSTO also refused to intervene in September 2022 after Armenia requested assistance to face Azerbaijani border. The organization also remained silent and inactive in the armed conflict opposing two of its members, Kyrgyzstan and Tajikistan in September 2022.

will not allow the scenario of the so-called color revolutions to be realized."[15] Labeling the January events as a failed "color revolution" is likely a way to underline foreign actors attempting to destabilize the region.

Conclusion

The literature suggests that in Kazakhstan, the government frequently blames Islamic radicals for unrest and also uses the threat of Islamic radicalism to discredit opponents and gain political legitimacy. The framing of the January 2022 events fits this discursive pattern. If state officials had not connected the events to foreign forces, they would have to recognize that the lootings and deaths during January occurred due to the failure of its social policies, thus, undermining their political legitimacy. In that particular case however, it was also used to request military assistance from the CSTO. The soldiery of CSTO could not have been drafted unless foreign forces threatened a member state. However, even though the government has not explicitly acknowledged its shortcomings, authorities moved forward with a number of reforms in the spring of 2022 (Sorbello, 2022a).

Protestors initially demanded to decrease the price of liquefied petroleum gas, remove former President Nazarbayev's hold over Kazakhstani politics, and a better representation of people's needs. Tokayev did initiate a series of reforms to correct some of the political and economic inequalities. For example, the price of gas was regulated, and petrol stations quickly started selling liquefied petroleum gas to its former price. The constitution saw a number of amendments after a referendum was held in June 2022. As a result, former President Nursultan Nazarbayev lost some of his privileges along with the status of "Elbasy" (the Head of Nation in Kazakh), the Constitutional Court will replace the Constitutional Council, and the Parliament (Mazhilis) will gain more power and presidential terms will be limited to one (Lillis, 2022b). Tokayev also announced early presidential elections in November and the Mazhilis in March 2023. In September 2022, President Tokayev signed a document returning the former name to the capital from Nur-Sultan to

[15] https://ria.ru/20220110/kazakhstan-1767129605.html.

Astana.[16] In a state-of-the-nation address on September 1, 2022, Tokayev announced a plan to foster a "Just and Fair Kazakhstan" which aims to "decentralize decision-making, strengthen the rule of law, increase international competitiveness, and ensure equal opportunities for every citizen" (Tokayev, 2022). For instance, it was decided to allocate 50 percent of the annual investment income of the National Fund to special savings accounts of young Kazakh residents until they reach the age of 18 (Tokayev, 2022). Tokayev also resigned from his position of the Chair of the ruling party, Amanat (formerly Nur-Otan), in order to put greater distance between the executive and legislative powers. There were also changes made to the electoral law to eliminate constraints on the registration and formation of political parties to promote political pluralism.

While these actions sound promising on paper, many scholars and observers are skeptical that the reforms will result in shaking the status quo that so many Kazakhstanis decried. The presidential administration has also remained relatively silent on issues of corruption that deprive Kazakhstanis of hundreds of millions of dollars every year and which were at the heart of the anger expressed in January. Even though Tokayev announced the creation of a commission charged with recovering money unlawfully taken out of the country, many are skeptical of its range of actions (Kumenov, 2022). From a political point of view, major changes are also not expected. Tokayev, who was elected President for the first time in June 2019, will run as a first-time candidate in the November 2022 election because of the Constitutional changes adopted this summer have technically put the counter back to zero. Whereas the maximum number of terms a President can serve has been limited to one, the length of the mandate has been extended from five to seven years, a change that will favor the current President who will, in total, be able to run the country for a period of 10 years, from 2019 until 2029. Despite the registration of new candidates, the current Presidential race is dominated by President Tokayev. For instance, the most well-known opposition

16 A name change he himself initially ordered in March 2019, one day after former President Nazarbayev resigned and Tokayev became interim President. This fawning decision was extremely unpopular in Kazakhstan and also costly. Even though the return to the original name was a welcomed decision, people underlined the absurdity of the whole affair.

parties, Ak Zhol and the People's Party, which normally present candidates in Presidential elections have covertly indicated that they would rally behind Tokayev (Sorbello, 2022b) and the other officially registered candidates are relatively unknown to the public. As of October 12, there were four candidates officially in the race. The first is Zhiguli Dayrabayev, a little-known member of the slightly better-known Auyl (Village) party, the second is Nurlan Auyesbayev of the National Social Democratic Party, the third is Meyram Kazhyken, an obscure academic and the fourth Karakat Abden, a female public figure, member of the National Commission for Women Affairs and Family and Democratic Policy (Lillis, 2022b). Eight potential candidates have pending applications and might also be approved after the Central Electoral Commission finishes to review their application and after candidates successfully pass the language test measuring one's proficiency of the Kazakh language.[17]

Despite a diversity of candidates, there is little doubt that Tokayev that will win the presidency. For thirty years, the Kazakhstani political system has been dominated by a clique that has prevented any serious political opposition figure to gain notoriety and a chance to democratically challenge incumbent leadership. Political change will take time. One peculiar aspect of this election will be the presence, for the first time ever, of a "Against all" option on the electoral ballot. Whereas in the past, voters might have been afraid of directly voting in favor of opposition candidates, now uninhibited Kazakhstanis might be tempted to voice their frustration and select this option. Election results, if presented honestly, will serve as a good barometer of people's trust in the political system.

References

Aaronson, S. A. (2017). *Repression, Civil Conflict and Leadership Tenure: A Case Study of Kazakhstan*. Institute for International Economic Policy-George Washington University.

Baisagatovaa, D., Kemelbekovb, S., Smagulovaa, D., & Kozhamberdiyevaa, A. (2016). Correlation of Concepts "Extremism" and "Terrorism" in Countering the Financing of Terrorism and Extremism. *International Journal of Environmental & Science Education, 11*(13), 5903–5915.

[17] https://www.agenzianova.com/en/news/Kazakhstan-12-nominations-for-the-seven-presidential-elections-awaiting-approval/.

BBC News. (2022, January 11). *Kazakhstan: Tokayev obivil o vyvode voisk ODKB I potreboval ot biznesa delitsa s narodom*. BBC News Russkaya Sluzba. https://www.bbc.com/russian/news-59952826. Accessed October 12, 2022.

Biuro natsionalnoi statistiki Agentstva po strategicheskomu planirovaniyu i reformam Respubliki Kazakhstan. (2022). *Itogi Natsional'noy perepisi naseleniya 2021 goda v Respublike Kazakhstan*. https://stat.gov.kz/api/getFile/?docId=ESTAT464825. Accessed October 12, 2022.

Cammett, M., & Jones, P. (2022). Illicit Economies and Political Violence in Central Asia. In *The Oxford Handbook of Politics in Muslim Societies (Oxford Handbooks)* (pp. 411–429). Oxford University Press.

Caron, J. F., & Malikova, V. (2021). Understanding Anti-Regime Activists' Failures During the 2019 Kazakhstan Presidential Election. *Understanding Kazakhstan's 2019 Political Transition*, 79–100. https://doi.org/10.1007/978-981-33-4308-5_5

Collective Security Treaty Organization. (1992). https://en.odkb-csto.org/documents/documents/dogovor_o_kollektivnoy_bezopasnosti/#loaded

Collective Security Treaty Organization. (2022, January 10). *10 yanvarya 2022 goda v formate videokonferentsii sostoyalos vneocherednaya sessiya Soveta kollektivnoy bezopasnosti ODKB. Obsuzhdalas situatsiya v Respublike Kazakhstan i mery po normalizatsii obstanovki v strane*. https://www.odkb-csto.org/session/2022/10-yanvarya-2022-goda-v-formate-videokonferentsii-sostoyalos-vneocherednaya-sessiya-soveta-kollektiv/#loaded. Accessed October 12, 2022.

Corsi, J. R. (1981). Terrorism as a Desperate Game. *Journal of Conflict Resolution, 25*(1), 47–85. https://doi.org/10.1177/002200278102500103

Elder, M. (2010, June 15). *Kyrgyzstan Tests Russia's Regional Commitments*. The World. https://theworld.org/dispatch/russia/100614/kyrgyzstan-ethnic-violence. Accessed October 12, 2022.

Heuer, V., & Hierman, B. (2022). Manhandling and Mediation: Unpacking the Repressive Repertoire in Kazakhstan's 2016 Anti-land Reform Protests. *Asian Security*, 1–18. https://doi.org/10.1080/14799855.2022.2034787

Karina, D. (2022, March 14). *В Казахстане не были 20 тысяч иностранных боевиков – Генпрокуратура*. Inbusiness.kz. https://inbusiness.kz/ru/last/v-kazahstane-ne-byli-20-tysyach-inostrannyh-boevikov-genprokuratura

Kudaibergenova, D. T., & Laruelle, M. (2022). Making Sense of the January 2022 Protests in Kazakhstan: Failing Legitimacy, Culture of Protests, and Elite Readjustments. *Post-Soviet Affairs*, 1–19. https://doi.org/10.1080/1060586x.2022.2077060

Kumenov, A. (2018, July 2). *Kazakhstan Is Throttling the Internet When the President's Rival Is Online*. Eurasianet. https://eurasianet.org/kazakhstan-is-throttling-the-internet-when-the-presidents-rival-is-online. Accessed September 22, 2022.

Kumenov, A. (2022, June 7). *Kazakhstan: President Vows to Stop Wealth Ending in Hands of "Narrow Circle"*. Eurasianet. https://eurasianet.org/kazakhstan-president-vows-to-stop-wealth-ending-in-hands-of-narrow-circle. Accessed October 12, 2022.

Libman, A., & Obydenkova, A. V. (2018). Understanding Authoritarian Regionalism. *Journal of Democracy, 29*(4), 151–165. https://doi.org/10.1353/jod.2018.0070

Lillis, J. (2022a, January 7). *Kazakhstan: Shoot to Kill Protesters, Orders Tough-Talking Tokayev*. Eurasianet. https://eurasianet.org/kazakhstan-shoot-to-kill-protesters-orders-tough-talking-tokayev. Accessed September 22, 2022.

Lillis. J. (2022b, October 6). *Kazakhstan: Business as Usual as One-Horse Race Looms in Presidential Vote*. Eurasianet. https://eurasianet.org/kazakhstan-business-as-usual-as-one-horse-race-looms-in-presidential-vote. Accessed October 22, 2022.

Lemon, E., & Thibault, H. (2018). Counter-Extremism, Power and Authoritarian Governance in Tajikistan. *Central Asian Survey, 37*(1), 137–159. https://doi.org/10.1080/02634937.2017.1336155

Lewis, D. (2016). Blogging Zhanaozen: Hegemonic Discourse and Authoritarian Resilience in Kazakhstan. *Central Asian Survey, 35*(3), 421–438. https://doi.org/10.1080/02634937.2016.1161902

Malashenko, A. (1994) Islam and Politics in the Southern Zone of the Former USSR. In V. V. Naumkin (Ed.), *Central Asia and Transcaucasia: Ethnicity and Conflict*. Greenwood Press.

Malik, B. A. (2019). Islam in Post-Soviet Kazakhstan: Experiencing Public Revival of Islam Through Institutionalisation. *Asian Journal of Middle Eastern and Islamic Studies, 13*(3), 351–369. https://doi.org/10.1080/25765949.2019.1630576

Matveeva, A. (2018). Radicalisation and Violent Extremism in Kyrgyzstan. *The RUSI Journal, 163*, 1.

Montgomery, D. W., & Heathershaw, J. (2016). Islam, Secularism and Danger: A Reconsideration of the Link Between Religiosity, Radicalism and Rebellion in Central Asia. *Religion, State and Society, 44*(3), 192–218. https://doi.org/10.1080/09637494.2016.1220177

Naumkin, V. V. (2005). *Radical Islam in Central Asia: Between Pen and Rifle*. Rowman & Littlefield.

Omelicheva, M. Y. (2011). Islam in Kazakhstan: A Survey of Contemporary Trends and Sources of Securitization. *Central Asian Survey, 30*(2), 243–256. https://doi.org/10.1080/02634937.2011.567069

Oxford Analytica. (2022, January 14). *Kazakh Leader Stronger But Unmet Promises Are a Risk*. https://dailybrief.oxan.com/Analysis/DB266681/Kazakh-leader-stronger-but-unmet-promises-are-a-risk

Radio Azattyq. (2022, January 29). *Prezident Kazakhstana otklonil prizyvy k mezhdunarodnomu rassledovaniyu yanvarskikh sobytiy*. Radio Azattyq. https://rus.azattyq.org/a/31677572.html. Accessed October 12, 2022.

Reshetnyak, A., & Omelicheva, M. (2022). A Framework for Explaining National P/CVE Programs: A Case Study of Kazakhstan. *Studies in Conflict & Terrorism*, 1–18. https://doi.org/10.1080/1057610x.2022.2090048

Sagadiyeva, A. (2021). *Social Taboos and Political Legitimation: Debating Polygyny in Post-Soviet Kazakhstan* (Master's Thesis). Nazarbayev University, Nur-Sultan. https://nur.nu.edu.kz/handle/123456789/5390. Accessed October 12, 2022.

Sailaubekuly, S. (2019). *Media and Power: Controlling Religion by Manipulating Public Opinion. The Case of Islam in Kazakhstan* (Master's Thesis). Nazarbayev University, Nur-Sultan. https://nur.nu.edu.kz/handle/123456789/3880. Accessed October 12, 2022.

Satpayev, D., & Umbetaliyeva, T. (2015). The Protests in Zhanaozen and the Kazakh Oil Sector: Conflicting Interests in a Rentier State. *Journal of Eurasian Studies, 6*(2), 122–129. https://doi.org/10.1016/j.euras.2015.03.005

Schatz, E. (2009). The Soft Authoritarian Tool Kit: Agenda-Setting Power in Kazakhstan and Kyrgyzstan. *Comparative Politics, 41*(2), 203–222. http://www.jstor.org/stable/40599210

Sharipova, D., & Beissembayev, S. (2021). Causes of Violent Extremism in Central Asia: The Case of Kazakhstan. *Studies in Conflict & Terrorism*, 1–21. https://doi.org/10.1080/1057610x.2021.1872163

Soliev, N. (2019). Central Asia: Kazakhstan, Kyrgyzstan, Tajikistan, Turkmenistan, Uzbekistan. *Counter Terrorist Trends and Analyses, 11*(1), 65–70. https://www.jstor.org/stable/26568579

Sorbello. P. (2022a, September 13). *Trials and Amnesties Continue as Kazakhstan Seeks Clarity About January*. Vlast. https://vlast.kz/english/51643-trials-and-amnesties-continue-as-kazakhstan-seeks-clarity-about-january.html. Accessed September 22, 2022.

Sorbello. P. (2022b, September 30). *The Week in Kazakhstan: Election Pessimists and Hydrocarbon Hopefuls*. Vlast. https://vlast.kz/english/51904-the-week-in-kazakhstan-election-pessimists-and-hydrocarbon-hopefuls.html Accessed October 12, 2022.

Stronski, P. (2016). *Kazakhstan at Twenty-five: Stable But Tense*. Carnegie Endowment for International Peace. https://carnegieendowment.org/2016/02/04/kazakhstan-at-twenty-five-stable-but-tense-pub-62642. Accessed October 12, 2022.

Thibault, H. (2018). *Transforming Tajikistan: State-Building and Islam in Post-Soviet Central Asia*. Bloomsbury Publishing.

Thibault, H. (2019). The Art of Managing Religion in a Post-Soviet Soft Authoritarian State. In *Kazakhstan and the Soviet Legacy* (pp. 155–179). Palgrave Macmillan.

Thibault, H. (2020). Political Islam in Central Asia: From Religious Revival to Securitization. In S. Akbarzadeh (Ed.), *Routledge Handbook of Political Islam* (pp. 139–154). Routledge.

Thibault, H. (2022) Where Did All the Wahhabis Go? The Evolution of Threat in Central Asian Scholarship. *Europe-Asia Studies, 74*(2), 288–309. https://doi.org/10.1080/09668136.2021.1999908

Tokayev, K.-J. (2022, September 20). *Kazakhstan's President: We're Moving Full Speed Ahead Toward Reform*. Politico. https://www.politico.eu/article/kazakh-president-we-must-flip-the-switch-of-reform/. Accessed October 12, 2022.

Tucker, N. (2018). What Happens When Your Town Becomes an ISIS Recruiting Ground? Lessons from Central Asia About Vulnerability, Resistance, and the Danger of Ignoring Perceived Injustice. *Central Asia Program Paper, 209*, 1–18.

Turgayev, S. (2022, January 13). *YA na ploshchadi ne videl terroristov. Protesty isportili provokatory*. Zhanbolat Mamay – o tom, kak mitingi v Almaty pererosli v "terakty." Nastoyashcheye Vremya. https://www.currenttime.tv/a/31650872.html. Accessed October 12, 2022.

Uyama, T. (2013). The Changing Religious Orientation of Qazaq Intellectuals in the Tsarist Period: Sharia, Secularism, and Ethics. In *Islam, Society and States Across the Qazaq Steppe* (pp. 95–117). Austrian Academy of Science.

Vlast. (2022, March 14). *Do 243 vyroslo chislo ugolovnykh del po faktam pytok zaderzhannykh posle yanvarskikh sobytiy*. Vlast. https://vlast.kz/novosti/49115-do-234-vyroslo-cislo-ugolovnyh-del-po-faktam-pytok-zaderzannyh-posle-anvarskih-sobytij.html. Accessed October 12, 2022.

Zhursyn, Z. (2022, January 5). *V Aktobe protestuyushchiye pytalis prorvatsya v akimat. Politsiya primenila slezotochivyy gaz*. Radio Azattyk. https://rus.azattyq.org/a/31640238.html. Accessed October 1, 2022.

Zhussipbek, G., Achilov, D., & Nagayeva, Z. (2020). Some Common Patterns of Islamic Revival in Post-Soviet Central Asia and Challenges to Develop Human Rights and Inclusive Society. *Religions, 11*(11), 548. https://doi.org/10.3390/rel11110548

Index

J.-F. Caron (ed.), *A Revolt in the Steppe*, The Steppe and Beyond: Studies on Central Asia,
https://doi.org/10.1007/978-981-99-0783-0

The manufacturer's authorised representative in the EU is Springer Nature Customer Service Centre GmbH, Europaplatz 3, 69115 Heidelberg, Germany. If you have any concerns regarding our products, please contact ProductSafety@springernature.com

Printed and bound by CPI Group (UK) Ltd, Croydon, CR0 4YY

01/10/2026

02225879-0001